INTER/NATIONALISM

INDIGENOUS AMERICAS
Robert Warrior, Series Editor

INTER/NATIONALISM

. . .

DECOLONIZING
NATIVE AMERICA AND
PALESTINE

. . .

STEVEN SALAITA

University of Minnesota Press
Minneapolis ▪ London

The author and the University of Minnesota Press are grateful for permission to reprint previously published poetry in chapter 4. Erica Violet Lee, "Our Revolution: First Nations Women in Solidarity with Palestine," was published on Moontime Warrior, http://moontimewarrior.com/. Carter Revard, "A Response to Terrorists," was published in *An Eagle Nation* (Tucson: University of Arizona Press, 1993), 101–2; copyright 1993 the Arizona Board of Regents; reprinted by permission of the University of Arizona Press. Lee Maracle, "Song to a Palestinian Child," was published in *Bent Box* (Penticon, British Columbia: Theytus, 2000), 33. Edgar Gabriel Silex, "Chief Nanay Appears in the Holy Land," was published in *Acts of Love* (Willimantic, Conn.: Curbstone Press, 2004), 33; copyright 2004 by Edgar Silex; all rights reserved. A translation of Mahmoud Darwish's "Red Indian's Penultimate Speech to the White Man," by Fady Joudah, was published in *Harvard Review* 36 (2009):152–59. Russell Means, "The Song of the Palestinian," was published in the blog The Corner Report.

Published by the University of Minnesota Press
111 Third Avenue South, Suite 290
Minneapolis, MN 55401-2520
http://www.upress.umn.edu

ISBN 978-1-5179-0141-7 (hc)
ISBN 978-1-5179-0142-4 (pb)
A Cataloging-in-Publication record for this title is available from the Library of Congress.

Printed in the United States of America on acid-free paper

The University of Minnesota is an equal-opportunity educator and employer.

22 21 20 19 18 17 16   10 9 8 7 6 5 4 3 2 1

For my parents, Miriam and Nasr

CONTENTS

INTRODUCTION

■   ■   ■

This book develops a theory of inter/nationalism, an amalgamation of what is sometimes called solidarity, transnationalism, intersectionality, kinship, or intercommunalism. I had no role in creating inter/nationalism. I have merely observed and subsequently named it. "Inter/nationalism" describes a certain type of decolonial thought and practice—not a new type of decolonialism, but one renewed vigorously in different strata of American Indian and Palestinian communities. At its most basic, inter/nationalism demands commitment to mutual liberation based on the proposition that colonial power must be rendered diffuse across multiple hemispheres through reciprocal struggle.

My goal in this book is to define, document, and advance bases for the scholarly and material comparison of American Indian and Palestinian societies. I imagine this project as both an activist and an intellectual document, though I am painfully aware that shortcomings of vision and execution are inevitable. Nevertheless, I hope the analysis I share will contribute to a larger movement seeking to conjoin radical thought within the academy to creative theorization beyond the academy's hermetic norms.

It is useful, if a bit obvious, to point out that the age of transnational humanities has arrived. No longer can scholars demarcate territories of intellectual pursuit based on the self-contained logic of linear group identity (those who feel they can, should not). Most of us would find that sort of provincialism undesirable even if it were a viable way of comprehending human relationships. Despite these ethical and methodological shifts, however, not enough has been written about the possibilities and implications of intercommunal scholarship or about the qualities of intercommunalism. *Inter/Nationalism* addresses these possibilities and implications, paying attention to dialectics between theorization and decolonial advocacy. More precisely, I explore the ability (or willingness) of scholarship to influence decolonial advocacy. At the very least I try to draw methodological inspiration from such advocacy. If theorists emerging from colonized or otherwise disenfranchised communities have thoroughly decimated the shibboleths of neutral or disengaged analysis, then I would like to examine what scholarship might accomplish when unburdened from the injunctions of objectivity.

America and Palestine are the geographies of primary interest. I have already written about both places. My book *The Holy Land in Transit* was published in 2006, but I compiled the majority of its research in the early 2000s. In the book, I look at some of the ways colonial discourses in North America and Palestine arise from the same moral and philosophical narratives of settlement, examining how modern Palestinian and Native literatures incorporate and react to those discourses.[1] Back then, there was good source material, some of which I had to mine from old documents, but the comparison of Native America and Palestine was limited. Robert Warrior had long before published his classic essay "Canaanites, Cowboys, and Indians" and the American Indian Movement had released numerous statements in support of Palestinian nationhood.[2]

Although I was not bereft of materials, over the past few years comparison of Natives and Palestinians has reached a level of sophistication and complexity I never could have imagined in 2006. This book is not meant to be a part two of *The Holy Land in Transit,* though they share obvious affinities. Rather, I conceptualize it as a synthesis of important comparative trends in American Indian studies and subsequently an analysis of the many roles Palestine plays in the development of ethics, innovations, and debates in American Indian studies, with a particular interest in theories of decolonization. This methodology enables us to move away from comparison of colonial discourses in order to explore the possibilities of comparing decolonial discourses. The shift seems simple, but it represents a significant methodological change, prioritizing matters of liberation rather than merely assessing the mechanics of colonization.

In situations of ongoing colonialism, geographic terminologies are simultaneously ambivalent and politicized (their ambivalence often results from their politicization; their politicization often arises from ambivalent affinities). I propose some definitional clarifications, if not definitions, in order to provide readers an understanding of the contexts in which I utilize ambivalent and politicized terms.

A good place to begin is with place-names, highly contentious signifiers often sanitized by assumptions of timeless neutrality. I considered for quite some time whether I would speak of "America," "the Americas," "the United States," or "North America." I ultimately selected "America," less for simplicity and more for its countless imaginative connotations. All nations, states, and territories are ideas and mythologies in addition to physical spaces, but the idea and myth of "America" resonate in distinctive ways as both a colonial archetype and a geography that traverse languages and borders. Although "America"—and any other identifier not belonging to a Native language—is a colonial locution, it is inclusive of North and South America as well as the Caribbean, regions whose decolonization (and colonization) is ongoing. Thus I would like to reimagine "America" as a hemispheric agglomeration of both discrete and interrelated Indigenous nations.

I have a primary interest in North America, the United States especially, and specify a focus on these regions (as others) where appropriate or necessary. When I refer to the United States, I am speaking of the colonial enterprise and subsequent nation-state, as opposed to the Indigenous spaces of America. The primary distinction here, beyond mere nomenclature, is the assignment of a concrete identifier to the nation-state that locks it into a particular historical condition as against an abstract, dynamic conceptualization of the hemisphere, that which precedes, and will outlast, the nation-state.

The naming of Palestine is simpler. I deploy "Palestine" to refer to the nation of Arabic-speaking Palestinian people—Muslim, Christian, Jewish, Druze, Samaritan, Baha'i, or atheist—with an origin in the historic land of Palestine, which includes today's Israel (minus the Golan Heights), the West Bank, and the Gaza Strip. While this population, as with other dispossessed people, has a global presence, its identity is intricately tied to its ancestral home, often deemed the Holy Land, a counterintuitive nomenclature given its histories of conflict. When I deploy the term "Israel," I refer to the colonial entity superimposed on the historic land of Palestine, an entity that continues a decades-long project of ethnic cleansing. "Israel" versus "Palestine" signifies a difference between the nation-state and the nation.

My usage of "decolonization/decolonize" is likewise simple, drawing from the common usage of the term throughout decades of scholarship. Frantz Fanon provides perhaps the most famous theory of decolonization in *The Wretched of the Earth* (a theory developed throughout his work):

> Decolonization, which sets out to change the order of the world, is clearly an agenda for total disorder. But it cannot be accomplished by the wave of a magic wand, a natural cataclysm, or a gentleman's agreement. Decolonization, we know, is an historical process: In other words, it can only be understood, it can only find its significance and become self coherent insofar as we can discern the history-making movement which gives it form and substance. Decolonization is the encounter between two congenitally antagonistic forces that in fact owe their singularity to the kind of reification secreted and nurtured by the colonial situation.[3]

Fanon's phrase "total disorder" does not denote chaos in the sense of a vanquished hierarchy or an absence of law. "Total disorder" describes a rejection of colonial rule and its socioeconomic precepts. It is the act of removing order from the structures of foreign authority. This removal of order is total because, according to Fanon, the colonial entity must be rejected completely, subverted, dismantled, decentralized—that is, dis-ordered.

Daniel
Rosa

7Lori
G visit
vs Carpesn

Mark - worship sharing

Just card
back
from
Sha

"Decolonization," Fanon concludes, "implies the urgent need to thoroughly challenge the colonial situation. Its definition can, if we want to describe it accurately, be summed up in the well-known words: 'The last shall be the first.' Decolonization is verification of this. At a descriptive level, therefore, any decolonization is a success."[4] The adage "the last shall be the first" announces a rearrangement of both fortune and circumstance. A sense of destiny—one evoked by the struggle for total disorder—also informs the adage. Fanon indicates that in addition to being pervasive, decolonization is inevitable. It is successful at a descriptive level for two primary reasons: once it is described, it is activated and thus irreversible; and it is in the performance and understanding of language that the native can begin the arduous process of psychic and political reimagination. Ultimately, for Fanon decolonization is less about physical resistance to foreign occupation and more about the psychological expulsion of the colonizer (a process that nevertheless can only occur through physical resistance).

It is this concept of decolonization to which I adhere, one refined and reformulated through the years by scholars such as Edward Said, Vine Deloria Jr., Gayatri Chakravorty Spivak, Samir Amin, Sunaina Maira, Mahmood Mamdani, Patrick Wolfe, and Neferti Tadiar. The decolonialist is wary of both the practices and self-image of modernity, a dynamic epoch roughly correlated to the rise of industrial capitalism; no community achieves the status of modern without the imprimatur of colonization. Decolonization aims to disrupt the interplay of colonial ethos with predominant conceptions of universal meaning and common sense. I use the term not simply to signify the process of expunging a foreign occupier from one's ancestral land, but also to identify the extirpation of a foreign occupier from one's economy, education system, and self-image.

In terms of disciplinary categories, the trickiness remains. A major theme of this project is the relationship of Palestine, as both a symbolic and a living space, with the field of American Indian studies (a broad field with degrees of overlap with Indigenous studies, Pacific Island studies, ethnic studies, and so forth). I usually highlight American Indian studies rather than the more general Indigenous studies not as an overt political decision but because the following chapters are mainly limited to North American nations. When I examine other areas of the world, I try to offer the appropriate nomenclature, though all taxonomies that describe Indigenous peoples are somehow contested, including the term "Indigenous." Indeed, one of my goals is to undermine the mechanical analyses of naming, which produce conversations fundamentally entrapped in the dictates of colonization, thereby impeding the invocation of more pressing questions. This goal is not intended to demean the importance of various modes of identification; rather, I suggest that naming usually consigns us to the realm of symbolism at the expense of intricate matters of liberatory dialogue and practice that render naming so complex and difficult in the first place—a situation arising from the peculiar juridical and discursive conventions of colonial practice.

As to inter/nationalism, it is not a term I presume to define, nor would I in any case consider a singular definition viable.

I use the term to emphasize action and dialogue across borders, both natural and geopolitical—not the nationalism of the nation-state, but of the nation itself, as composed of heterogeneous communities functioning as self-identified collectives attached to particular land bases. Inter/nationalism is a way to compare nationalisms, to put them into conversation, but also to examine how the invention and evolution of national identities necessarily rely on international dialectics. An interesting conversation developing in American Indian studies centers on the role of Palestine in the field, the nucleus of this book. I am not merely interested in elucidating the processes by which Palestine has become a topic of interest in American Indian studies, although I will do that, but also in exploring the implications of incorporating Palestine into the discipline and the comparative possibilities that exist when it happens.

This usage of "inter/nationalism" both resumes and shifts the notion of the international and internationalism in left political traditions, socialism especially. Internationalism in these traditions often traces to the nonaligned movement and the anticolonial struggles of the global South. It also has a significant presence in radical black organizing in the United States and the Caribbean.

Socialist (and, to a lesser degree, anarchist) internationalism is critical to our ability to render the backslash to "inter/nationalism" more intelligible and specific. That backslash locates emphasis in a particular sort of struggle pertaining to the conditions of decolonization in worldwide Indigenous communities, though in this book it emerges in relation to Natives and Palestinians.

A central tenet of inter/national scholarship is insistence on transnational dialogue not only extraneous, but in opposition to the physical and legal parameters of the nation-state. Inherent to that tenet is commitment to the well-being of Indigenous nations based on the terms of their own communal needs and values. While it might be hyperbolic to say that all Indigenous peoples will have to be liberated simultaneously, it can be observed that a discrete power structure, of which the United States and Israel are primary stewards and beneficiaries, maintains their dispossession. That power structure preserves its existence through pervasive reinvention based on the common sense of divine intendment, which manifests itself at the levels of assumption and praxis in cultural, educational, governmental, and legal institutions. Indigenous struggles for liberation exist at the axis of what it means to contest empire, militarism, and economic injustice. The actions and ideas of today's Indigenous scholars and activists highlight the importance of inter/national theory and analysis, which I consider more carefully in the following paragraphs, paying note to how it encompasses both the ideological and the material.

Inter/nationalism encourages and assesses the play of decolonial narratives across cultures and colonial borders. I divide the term with a slash to reflect not just the political, philosophical, and ethical dialogue intimated by the prefix "inter," but also to separate "nationalism" from the prefix while keeping the two halves connected in such a way that they create more possibilities in juxtaposition. Inter/nationalism expresses a desire for scholarship to explore broader patterns of discourse and power in our analyses of specific communities and a commitment to the project of nation building through deep engagement with decolonial paradigms. Whereas "internationalism," without the slash, connotes cosmopolitan modernity or an epistemology of worldly experience, "inter/nationalism," with its typographical emphasis on the complex and volatile term "nationalism," encourages the possibility of putting nationalisms into conversation or, more ambitiously, into collective practice. Whereas in *The Holy Land in Transit* I work with the term "reciprocal communalism," I lately decided that it does not offer quite the precision I seek. The notion of reciprocity is crucial, as is emphasis on community, but "communalism" does not expressly underscore the nation, a problem solved, conspicuously, with the word *nationalism,* despite its ambiguities.

I adhere to a notion of nationalism generally accepted in American Indian studies, the one articulated by Jace Weaver, Craig Womack, and Robert Warrior in *American Indian Literary Nationalism,* with Simon Ortiz's thoughts on the subject serving as their foundation: "It is because of the acknowledgment by Indian writers of a responsibility to advocate for their people's self-government, sovereignty, and control of land and natural resources; and to look also at racism, political and economic oppression, sexism, supremacism, and the needless and wasteful exploitation of land and people . . . that Indian literature is developing a character of nationalism."[5] The preface to Weaver, Womack, and Warrior's book declares, "Nationalism is a term on a short list, one that also includes sovereignty, culture, self-determination, experience, and history, that is central to understanding the relationship between the creative expression of Native American literature and the social and historical realities that such expression embodies."[6] This formulation avoids the kind of nationalism, born of the industrial revolution, that so often goes hand in hand with jingoism, patriotism, and imperialism, highlighting instead a descriptive symbol of geography and humanity, the nation, not as constituted in the image of the Western state but in a dynamic structure of discrete, autonomous community (that exists in permanent contestation to the Western state). The nation in this scenario is a collective that works in the interests of community rather than of corporations and plutocrats. It precedes the nationalism of state-sponsored patriotism.

Nationalism relates to inter/nationalism in varied and important ways. The nation is not an isolated organism. It is a radical entity that survives in relation to the destinies of other nations, especially in this era of decolonization. It was disassembled in the era of poststructuralism, but retains profound value to Natives and Palestinians as a subject of cultural practice, not merely as a geo-political, historical, or discursive entity. Conceptualizing the nation as a subject of cultural practice compels us to consider the implications of peoplehood in the framework of liberation, while tending to the effects on identity when a displaced group endeavors to repossess the autonomies of its precolonial existence.

Native and Indigenous support of, and participation in, the Boycott, Divestment, and Sanctions (BDS) movement constitutes a quintessential form of inter/nationalism. (I examine BDS in great detail in chapter 2.) Other examples include the solidarity work among Palestinians and Hawaiians;[7] the participation of Palestine activists in Idle No More; the conjoining of Native and Palestinian scholars in the spaces of critical ethnic studies; the steady migration of Palestine scholars from Middle East studies into various areas of Indigenous studies; the repositioning of Palestinians into the category of Indigenous at the United Nations and other international governing bodies;[8] and the increasingly common juxtaposition of Natives and Palestinians in all areas of the American and Israeli political spectrums. Each phenomenon provides a strong basis for inter/national scholarship of the variety that both harnesses and contributes to the work of decolonization occurring inside and beyond academe. The opportunity to examine Natives and Palestinians as agents of decolonization rather than limiting ourselves to the colonial discourses of the United States and Israel offers a crucial paradigm shift in the development of comparative methodologies, reorienting emphasis from the state to the nation.

Before I enter into these analyses, I offer a final qualification, one that highlights the limits of inter/national work. While there is much to support the effectiveness of comparative scholarship and to support intercommunal approaches for theory, activism, service, and pedagogy, there are problems inherent to comparing cultural practice rather than examining contexts of intellectual and historical interchange across the restrictive categories of academic labor and the physical constraints of geopolitical borders. I am wary of moves that, even inadvertently, compartmentalize the complexities of formal and informal cultural practice into comprehensible phenomena sorted within the taxonomies of Western epistemology.

To make my point simpler, one could spend plenty of time showing how, say, Palestinian and Ojibwe, or Cherokee and Maori, cultures are similar—and "culture" itself is an intangible term—but such a move risks evoking the dredges of an antiquated cultural anthropology. I would suggest, then, that it is a mistake to orient comparative scholarship around the ceremonial or the spiritual and look instead at sets of historicized encounters made in the past or that have the potential to happen in the future. I do not offer this argument as a universal suggestion, for there are ways that the spiritual can transcend hermetic practice, but as a way to identify a need for contextual precision in our approaches to the inter/national. Similarity can be an interesting basis for scholarship, but it often limits us to justifications for comparison rather than illuminating the range of dialectical possibility. In the following chapters, I aim to fulfill that goal.

Questions arise about the conduct and modalities of inter/national work; those questions will need to be addressed and readdressed as inter/nationalism continues to influence American Indian and Indigenous studies. In order to function optimally, the starting point of inter/nationalist methodologies, in both research and political organizing, must be sincere commitment to solidarity, to use a quaint term, one I prefer to similar possibilities: affinity, fraternity, unity, interconnection, fellowship, alliance (terms that actually describe the relationship between the United States and Israel). Solidarity, though overused and subsequently attenuated in public discourse, can be distinguished from comparable terms because it implies pursuit of common goals—in this case, a common future—rather than appealing to the abstract tenets of existential amity. Even granting that this distinction arises from my own interpretive preference, the broader point is that whatever we call the practices of inter/nationalism, they are better suited to decolonial aspirations than to cosmopolitan dialogue.

Solidarity requires certain ethical commitments to function. A functional solidarity does not involve appropriation. It does not come with the expectation of reciprocity. It is not quid pro quo. It is not recorded on ledgers. Solidarity is performed in the interest of better human relationships and for a world that allows societies to be organized around justice rather than profit. It happens across the communities with whom we are in contact—on behalf of the many we have never met.

Without the idea of Palestine, North America might have been conquered in much different fashion. And without that conquest, Israel might have been but a fleeting historical experiment, a new Republic of Ararat or State of Aleppo. Natives and Palestinians, then, have much to discuss. The first order of business is the acknowledgment that all peoples of America and Palestine must, of geopolitical necessity, be liberated together, and that our scholarship should be an asset toward that goal, not a mere recapitulation of state power.

1.
HOW PALESTINE BECAME IMPORTANT TO AMERICAN INDIAN STUDIES

◾   ◾   ◾

In the nascent days of the millennium, I was a new doctoral student at the University of Oklahoma, attempting to convince potential dissertation committee members of the utility of my proposed project, a comparison of the discourses of colonization in North America and Palestine. It was a difficult sell. The person who would direct my dissertation, Alan Velie, was easygoing, telling me to work on whatever suited me, but other faculty worried that the idea would be too broad or mechanical. Those concerns would later play a critical role in my attempts to manage the focus of the project. Like nearly all doctoral students, I was deeply anxious about my ability to even compose a dissertation. I knew that I knew too little to know how to adequately respond to skeptical authority figures with much greater knowledge.

Eminent scholar Robert Warrior joined the faculty before my third year. I immediately approached him, though with considerable apprehension, not knowing much about his politics or predilections. He expressed enthusiasm about the idea, explaining to me his history with Edward Said and his experiences living and working in Palestine.[1] It quickly became evident in my conversations with Warrior that his interest in my project amounted to more than a corresponding interest in the Middle East. It was also methodological. Warrior existed, and continues to exist, at an intersection of variegated, intercommunal methodologies, a focus extending from his first book, *Tribal Secrets,* to the magisterial volume *The World of Indigenous North America.* This twenty-year period in American Indian studies saw increased focus on the national traditions of individual tribes but also on expansive practices of transnational communication. As I became immersed in the field, I realized that American Indian studies has performed inter/nationalism since its inception, a necessity given the heterogeneity of Indigenous nations in America. Descriptions of this transnational focus include "intertribal" and the all but obsolete "pan-Indian," but in recent years inquiry in the field has moved beyond tribalism (in the sense of Darcy McNickle's usage) and assessment of pannational affinities, though those subjects remain important.[2] Recent scholarship has exhibited interest in the histories, politics, and cultures of a wide range of non-American geography. For example, American Indian studies has recently forged connections with Palestine at an institutional level—that is, scholars in the field are now producing systematic analyses of Palestine as a geography of interest (and in some ways crucial) to our understanding of decolonization in North America. How does the presence of Palestine in the field shape and define its limits and possibilities? What are the terms and frameworks for useful comparative scholarship? Are there material politics at stake in comparing America and Palestine? This chapter analyzes those questions.

Before I sort out the comparative bases of Natives and Palestinians, let us take a look at some of the reasons comparison of Natives and Palestinians has increased in recent years. I believe there are three primary factors, each with its own set of contradictions and subtexts:

1. The proliferation of blogs and social media where people are able to argue, inform, share, and theorize, however superficially (or, in some cases, sophisticatedly). These platforms lend themselves to all sorts of comparisons, usually for the sake of rhetorical persuasion. The benefits

and detriments of social media to activism and scholarship are wide-ranging and in much contest, so it is difficult to quantify the exact level of influence of new media on the surge of comparison among Natives and Palestinians, but social media platforms document the extent to which the comparison has entered into the consciousness of a certain demographic, that of the intellectual engaged in public discourse around decolonization.

2. Palestine scholars and activists increasingly use the language of Indigeneity and geocultural relationships to describe the political, economic, and legal positions of Palestinians. For instance, in referencing Natives and Palestinians, Sa'ed Adel Atshan speaks of "our shared history as Indigenous peoples who have faced ethnic cleansing by European colonists."[3] The adoption of such language is a rhetorical act meant to situate—rightly, based on considerable evidence—Palestinian dispossession in a specific framework of colonial history rather than as an exceptional set of events brought forth by ahistorical circumstances. The language identifies a perceived sociohistorical familiarity with other dispossessed communities, in this case North American indigenes. The declaration that Palestinians are not merely native or original but *indigenous* to the land colonized by Israel, not a completely new phenomenon but one growing in frequency, alters a number of crucial factors of Palestinian strategies of decolonization, in particular the relationship of human rights organizations with international law, the comparative possibilities in fields such as ethnic and Indigenous studies, and both intellectual and physical deployment of Palestinian nationalism into transnational spaces.

3. The most important reason for the proliferation of comparative discourses is the Boycott, Divestment, and Sanctions movement (BDS). Boycott of Israeli institutions or of the state itself has a long, albeit uneven, history in

the Arab world. When I discuss BDS, I have in mind a specific call for cultural and academic boycott issued in 2005 by nearly two hundred organizations representing Palestinian civil society.[4] Thus BDS is not a governmental or corporate initiative, but neither is it spontaneous or organic, for it arises from a long history of decolonial advocacy on an international scale. Narrowly, BDS can be identified as an initiative of Palestinian civil society to pressure the Israeli state to comply with international laws against colonialism and military occupation, using nonviolent methods of resistance as opposed to traditional diplomatic and dialogic strategies that have repeatedly failed (peace talks, for example, or multicultural programming). This movement continues to grow. What does BDS have to do with American Indian studies? A great deal, actually. I will explain the connections in more detail in chapter 2, but briefly, many Native scholars and activists have taken up the cause of BDS and in so doing have broadened the conditions of studying the decolonization of America and deepened what it means to undertake the types of intellectual and political activities one might perform in the service of Palestinian liberation.

Other reasons for the increase in comparisons of Natives and Palestinians include the ascension of Palestine as a test case of one's decolonial/leftist/scholarly credibility; the success of the Palestinian national movement in convincing greater numbers of people around the world to support or even identify with its cause (aided by increased Israeli belligerence and its dissemination in alternative media); the growth of Arab American studies, a field to which Palestine is central, in the academic spaces of ethnic studies, where it has encountered American Indian and Indigenous studies; and the increased emphasis in American Indian and Indigenous studies on transnational and comparative methodologies, which has led numerous scholars from the Pacific, North America, and South America to Palestine both intellectually and physically.

In early 2012, a small delegation of U.S.-based scholars visited Palestine, a visit arranged by the United States Academic and Cultural Boycott of Israel (USACBI), which campaigns for various BDS initiatives and helps set policy around ethical forms of boycott. In the past few decades, delegations to the West Bank and/or Gaza have been common, usually undertaken by peace groups or students. (Delegations arranged by Zionist organizations to Israel are likewise common; these delegations usually enjoy better funding and attendance.) The 2012 delegation, conceptualized in part as a fact-finding mission, differed from typical delegations in that it was peopled by prominent scholars with expertise in various areas of race and ethnicity. The point of view of the delegation, then, went beyond gathering information that would justify BDS. It also situated Palestinian dispossession in a framework of worldwide neoliberal practices, rather than merely as a consequence of communal strife or historical misfortune. The group was influenced by analysis of iniquity located primarily within U.S. racial paradigms. As a result, we have available an example of how Palestine can be of interest to American Indian studies, in this case through inter/national analysis performed by multiethnic and interdisciplinary academics.

Upon return, one of the delegates, Neferti X. M. Tadiar, observed:

> Palestinian life is . . . not the accomplishment of one aberrant state, inasmuch as the latter is supported by a global economy and geopolitical order, which condemns certain social groups and strata to the status of absolutely redundant, surplus populations—an order of insatiable accumulation and destruction that affects all planetary life. The question of Palestine is thus an urgent question of a just and equitable future that is both specific to this context and to this people, and a general and paradigmatic global concern.[5]

Another delegate, J. Kēhaulani Kauanui, reflects on a critical conversation she had about BDS in Haifa with a group of Palestinian citizens of Israel:

> What emerged from the conversation was that '48 Palestinians are attempting to shift the discourse to the paradigm of settler

colonialism emerging from their concern with the general framework of discourse around the Palestinian question. This approach to boycott insists on a reframing to open up connections with all Palestinians. I could relate to this. In my work fighting the US occupation of Hawai'i, I routinely challenge the US government's legal claim to Hawai'i, expose the roots of the US as a settler colonial state, and critically engage the history of US imperialism in Native America and the Pacific Islands, insisting on the recognition of US empire as a form of violent, global domination.[6]

Both Tadiar and Kauanui emphasize Palestine as a global issue. Tadiar in particular contests what might be called the regionalization of the Israel–Palestine conflict—that is, the propensity to view (by design or ignorance) the conflict as limited to the regional circumstances of its creation. Kauanui personalizes Palestine, reflecting on her history as a scholar-activist of Hawaiian liberation to enter into better comprehension of Zionism's pervasive colonial history. Both writers make clear the need to approach Palestine as a crucial site of global struggle, in the process inherently acknowledging the importance—indeed, centrality—of American decolonization to that struggle.

The delegation visited Palestine at a salient historical moment and in turn played a critical role in developing that moment into something consequential and sustainable. It was conceived amid a growing awareness of Palestine as a nexus of inter/national possibility, a place where one can encounter the self-perpetuating incarnations of U.S. history. The professors who traveled from America to Palestine illustrated that scholarship limited to the environs of the campus usually overlooks the worldly knowledge in abundance in places whose subjugation enables the accrual of educational status and wealth—such places where so many work so hard to conceptualize status and wealth as a natural condition.

The New New Canaan

There are particular conditions in which Native scholars have taken up the issue of Palestine. The possibilities of comparison are tremendously rich and accommodate complicated sites of material politics (by which I mean economic systems, activist communities, electoral processes, educational paradigms, and modes of resistance). Accessing those sites enables us to aspire to relationships that go beyond theoretical innovation by concomitantly emphasizing the practices and possibilities of decolonization. If early settlers conceptualized North America as a New Canaan (in perpetual evidence by the numerous towns across the United States with biblical nomenclature), then the role Israel plays in American imperial practices extends the metaphor by using the immutable legitimacy of its colonial enterprise as further justification for the permanence of a federal United States under whose ultimate jurisdiction Indigenous nations will remain. America thus becomes a New Canaan all over again, invigorated by the emergence of a nation-state atop the original Canaan.

Although North America was settled by different national groups, colonization of the so-called New World has been infused with a particular narrative of salvation, redemption, and destiny. Settlers assumed the role of Joshua crossing the river Jordan into Canaan, where God commanded them to exterminate the Indigenous populations and establish for themselves a beatific nation on a land of milk and honey underused and unappreciated by the natives.[7] The English, Puritans most specifically, were the most avid proponents of this view, but vast geographies of North America were overwhelmed by settlers and missionaries animated by godly purpose. Even in acknowledging the variegated, often conflicting, narratives of New World settlement, multitudinous sources illustrate that from its earliest moments, the United States has been beholden to a Holy Land ethos, articulated in various ways throughout the enterprise of European settlement.[8]

The emergence of Zionism in Europe in the late nineteenth century evoked a dialectic with the project of American settlement that remains today in the close relationship between the United States and Israel, apparent in military aid, security cooperation, and foreign policy. However, it is actually in the complex discursive and psychological spaces of ideology that the two states most closely align. The relationship is built through particular articulations of belonging that codify national identity into the mythologies of colonial domination and military conquest. Both Israel and the United States are relentlessly exceptional—and they are exceptional, ironically, only together.

Through identification and assessment of those connections, scholars in American Indian studies have made important advances in modes of analysis that inform my inter/national rubric. For instance, there has been much reflection on the relationship of Zionism with global systems of imperialism, militarization, plutocracy, and the neoliberal economies that undercut Indigenous self-determination in numerous parts of the world. U.S. support for Israel tells us much about the breadth of actors and actions involved in the continued occupation of Native lands in North America. Israel's conduct in the world, beyond its mistreatment of Palestinians, affects the health and economies of Indigenous communities worldwide, Indian country among them. Israel participates in the neoliberal corruption that dispossesses Natives of land and resources. Orly Benjamin's "Roots of the Neoliberal Takeover in Israel" illustrates the origins and consequences of Israel's neoliberalism, which partly explains the state's contribution to repression and genocide of Indigenous peoples in Guatemala and El Salvador in the 1980s. As a variety of scholars and journalists have shown, that contribution included logistical oversight and material support.[9] General Efraín Ríos Montt, architect of Guatemala's 1982–83 genocide, which especially affected Ixil communities in the country's highlands, considered Israel an indispensable ally in the global fight against communism, with which he fancifully associated Guatemala's Native communities.

When we think of Israel's effect on American policy, Indigenous communities rarely figure into the conversation, yet, as with the vast majority of state-sponsored or corporate perfidy, Indigenous communities are the ones who most suffer the immanence of iniquity. Latin America is a noteworthy site of Israeli perfidy, which, in keeping with the practice of neoliberal geopolitics, has disproportionately harmed Natives (along with the poor more broadly). Many reasons exist for this disproportionate harm. In general, plutocratic conduct, as Jodi Byrd, Jasbir Puar, and Scott Morgensen illustrate, exists in contradistinction to the practice of Indigenous self-determination.[10] Plutocracy invariably dispossesses Indigenous peoples and further impoverishes them through resource appropriation, military occupation, environmental destruction, and sponsorship of neocolonial corruption.

Israel's covert activities in Latin America have also directly harmed Indigenous peoples. Those activities occur in the framework of U.S. imperialism, for which Israel often acts as interlocutor. Israel likewise offers its police and military for hire as consultants to both industrial and developing states, in some cases supplying arms or tactical support.[11] Israel's most recent foray into Latin America has involved Mexico, although, as Jimmy Johnson and Linda Quiquivix reveal, "Mexico began receiving Israeli weaponry in 1973 with the sale of five Arava planes from Israel Aerospace Industries. Throughout the 1970s and '80s, infrequent exports continued to the country in the form of small arms, mortars and electronic fences. Sales escalated in the early 2000s, according to research that we have undertaken."[12] Today Israel provides Mexico with training and weapons in its counterinsurgency against the (Mayan) Zapatistas in Chiapas. Zapatista leader Rafael Guillén Vicente (aka Subcomandante Insurgente Marcos) has noted Israel's role as a colonial aggressor across the Atlantic: "Not far from here, in a place called Gaza, in Palestine, in the Middle East, right here next to us, the Israeli government's heavily trained and armed military continues its march of death and destruction."[13]

If Gaza, in Marcos's formulation, is "right next" to Chiapas, then it also abuts significant parts of Central America. Israel's role in the 1982–83 genocide of Mayans in Guatemala was more than peripheral. It supplied arms, many captured from the Palestine Liberation Organization (PLO), to the Honduran and Guatemalan governments.[14] In Guatemala it offered counterinsurgency training and military logistics. Rodolfo Lobos Zamora, the chief of staff of the Guatemalan army during the 1980s, proclaimed, "The Israeli soldier is the model for our soldiers."[15] In 1982, Montt, then Guatemala's president, "told ABC News that his success was due to the fact that 'our soldiers were trained by Israelis.'"[16] During the 2013 genocide trial of Montt, a charge of which he was convicted, further evidence of Israeli involvement came to light, including the Guatemalan army's use of helicopters supplied by Israel in addition to various intelligence channels, whose establishment led to the widespread torture and imprisonment of activists and civilians.[17]

Israel has also been implicated as a U.S. proxy in Africa, South Asia, and South America (in addition to numerous locales throughout the Arab world). Whatever role the United States plays in fomenting worldwide unrest or the codification of servitude, Israel is a ready tool or proxy, if not directly then certainly as what might be called a satellite surrogate of U.S. foreign policy. The disproportionate modes of dispossession that Indigenous peoples, American Indians particularly, experience because of U.S. and Israeli colonization show that philosophical and spiritual identifications between the United States and Israel have produced numerous material consequences for Indians in addition to the more conspicuous victims, the Palestinians. It is worth mentioning that while Israeli military and strategic assistance to Central American autocrats explicitly harms Indigenous peoples, there is much evidence to suggest that Natives in the United States also are victimized by Israel's close ties to the United States, primarily through neoliberal trade and development that pillage resources and limit economic development to the framework of profit-obsessed capitalism rather than allowing for the practice of legitimate egalitarian principles. Israel profits from neoliberalism at the expense of indigenes.

Resettling the Unsettled State

The vast majority of Jewish settlers to Palestine until 1967 were from Europe and the Arab world. The movement to settle the West Bank (and at various points the Gaza Strip and Sinai Peninsula) gained momentum in the 1970s and has not slowed, in large part based on U.S. influence—not merely in terms of the financial and political support proffered by the U.S. government, but in terms of the nationality of many of the settlers. In 2011 WikiLeaks published diplomatic cables from the U.S. consular office in Tel Aviv. The State Department officers "found that the U.S. citizens' reasons for moving to Jewish settlements in the area where Palestinians hope to establish a state were three-fold: social, economic, and ideological."[18]

The social factors include the opportunity to live in a largely isolated community with like-minded neighbors under heavy guard by the Israel Defense Forces (IDF). The economic advantages include tax breaks, subsidized loans, charity from evangelical Christians, and easy commutes to the green line on segregated roads. (The settlement of Elkana even provides schoolchildren free busing to ultraright-wing rallies.) The ideological phenomena are of primary concern, although there is no element of social and economic life in a settlement unaffected by ideology. The diplomatic cables conceptualize ideology in this instance as messianic fervor, of which many settlers are certainly possessed, but we can examine it in broader contexts of discourse, identity, and mythology.

Much of the current West Bank settler discourse emerges from U.S. history and bears hallmarks of North American racialist jurisprudence. It likewise recapitulates the same myths of divine purpose endemic to U.S. self-esteem. In fact, many American settlers to the West Bank, approximately 15 percent of the total settler population, self-identify as liberal, according to the research of Sara Hirschhorn, who was profiled in the Israeli daily *Ha'aretz*:

> "Jewish-American immigrants [to the territories] were primarily young, single, and highly identified as Jewish or traditional but not necessarily Orthodox in their religious orientation," Hirschhorn said. "They were primarily political liberals in the United States, voted for the Democratic Party and have been active in 1960s radicalism in the United States, participating in the Civil Rights Movement and the struggle against the Vietnam War."[19]

The *Ha'aretz* profile continues:

> Many Americans who moved to the settlements after the Six-Day War see what they're doing in Israel as an extension of their radicalism in the United States, Hirschhorn said. "They would also say that what some of them consider what they're doing in the territories in part as an expression of their own Jewish civil rights."

"In coming to Israel and participating in the settlement movement these American Jews continued in their radicalism," the Massachusetts native said. "While many others from their generation went back to a more conventional lifestyle—becoming soccer mommies and moving to Scarsdale [an affluent New York suburb]—here they moved to a hilltop on the West Bank."

Hirschhorn added that many Americans who move to the West Bank are trying to recapture the pioneering idealism of the state's Zionist founders, while others are driven by a Biblical imperative to settle the land.[20]

Hirschhorn, like earlier scholars, concludes that only a small portion of American West Bank settlers are overtly motivated by messianism. The majority of those settlers consider messianism secondary or unrelated to their presence in Palestine.

The term "messianism" requires consideration. Hirschhorn's usage appears to be synonymous with "a Biblical imperative to settle the land," which is generally accurate, although the term can also describe any sort of fervor of an intransigent variety. In both senses of the term, the self-identified liberal settlers who supposedly eschew messianism in fact practice it. In some ways they embody it. By settling a foreign land while claiming adherence to humanistic principles, they actually intensify (through the uncompromising assumptions of exclusion) the notion that Palestine is a land belonging to people who are not Palestinian.

It would be easy to theorize a discrepancy between the settlers' stated commitment to civil rights and their messianism, but the two attitudes actually align. Let us focus on the belief that settlement of Palestine is "an expression of their own Jewish civil rights," which is not as ridiculous as it first appears. The liberal discourses of American multiculturalism allow for expression of both colonial desire and communal racism because those discourses are devoted to the modern logic of individualism—the process by which racism is consigned to individualistic failure or ignorance rather than being located in the institutions of the colonial state. Furthermore, it has long been a contention across the Zionist political spectrum that Israel is a national embodiment of Jewish culture. If this is the case (and here I submit that national identity is never a complete representation of organic culture), then rejection or even contestation of Zionism becomes an act of cultural insensitivity, susceptible to charges of anti-Semitism or intolerance.

This rationale not only protects Israel from criticism, it also allows the settlers to conceptualize their presence on the West Bank as cultural performance, unburdened by violence or aggression. If Israel is the material outcome of Jewishness, then there is no contradiction in professing support for U.S. minorities and simultaneously effecting Palestinian dispossession, for the Palestinians are merely unfortunate bystanders in a Judeocentric drama of very recent vintage, but one that precedes them in imagination. Being liberal (in the modern U.S. sense of the term) offers a terrific basis for a concerned citizen to evolve into an ideologue with the power to summon for personal use the vast weaponry of a militarized nation-state. Messianic narratives, even when unclaimed, demand that sort of evolution.

American Indians too are an inconvenient impediment to a project much grander than their earthly lives. It is worth noting that the West Bank settlers' support of U.S. minorities does not extend to Indigenous self-determination—in U.S. discourses, it rarely does. Everywhere in the United States we see the interplay of liberalism (informed by unacknowledged messianism) with settler-colonial values of permanent entitlement (to land, to access, to belonging, to upward mobility—in short, to all the spoils of conquest, without having to assume responsibility for its immorality). Perhaps this phenomenon is nowhere more evident than in the controversies over Devils Tower in Wyoming. Known by Natives as Mato Tipila and sacred to the Lakota and other nations, Devils Tower is a hot spot for recreational climbers, who pound metal into the rock face and interfere with religious rituals.

Unsuccessful in their bid to outlaw climbing on Devils Tower, Natives have been treated to fantastic displays of liberal colonial logic. Frank Sanders, for example, was deeply concerned with the plight of Indians. "The Native Americans need physical help," he explained to *Climbing* writer Luke Laeser. "We have been working with the clinic at the Porcupine Reservation bringing them very basic supplies (things that you and I take for granted)."[21] In turn, in 2007–8 Sanders undertook Project 365, where he would climb Devils Tower every day for a year, helping to raise money for needy Indians. Asserting the sacredness of the site to himself, he later founded www.devilstowersacredtomanypeople.org.[22] In climbing Devils Tower for 365 days in a row, Sanders aimed to end Indian poverty and create an interracial harmony unseen in the region since the first days of European contact.

The only thing Natives asked of him was to quit desecrating Mato Tipila.

Agency and Appropriation

Recent work in inter/national analysis has brought forth two important advances. The first is the transformation of Native peoples from complex political subjects into metaphorical objects of decolonial credibility. To put it more simply, Indians have become actors in the rhetorical battlegrounds of the Israel—Palestine conflict. Zionists say: Jews are like the Indians.[23] Palestinians say: nonsense, we are. Both Zionists and anti-Zionists recognize in Indians a sort of moral authority on the subject of dispossession with which they seek to be associated. I should pause for a moment to note that I find numerous problems with the formulation. I am identifying it as a phenomenon, common these days, rather than endorsing it.

My main problem with these appeals to Native authority as a way to accrue decolonial legitimacy is simple: neither Zionists nor anti-Zionists need to be correct for anything to change in our understanding of Palestine, not to mention our understanding of America (which gets trivialized and dehistoricized in this type of situation). Indeed, the historical dispossession of Indians has often resembled, and in some instances has more than resembled, the mistreatment of Jews, particularly in Spain on the eve of Columbus's voyage and in Eastern Europe after the industrial revolution. But these realities do not preclude Palestinian dispossession from also resembling that of Indians. In fact, Palestinian dispossession also often resembles historical Jewish dispossession; that the Palestinians' current oppressors self-identify as Jewish does not diminish this simple fact of history. Thus the crude comparisons made for the sake of rhetorical expediency stop short of analyzing the historical, economic, and discursive forces that inform the U.S.–Israeli alliance and bind Natives and Palestinians to the same anticolonial polity.

The second thing that comes out of these advances in inter/national analysis is what we learn about the practice of American Indian studies as an academic enterprise that exists beyond the corridors of academe, by which I mean the element of the field, not always consistent but omnipresent, that compels its participants to practice communal engagement and pursue social justice (to use an old-fashioned term, one that might interchange with human rights, sovereignty, self-determination, liberation, and so forth). This ethic, in contradistinction to the traditional notion of scholars as practitioners of an objective vocation, is apparent in the mission statements of numerous academic departments. The Native American and Indigenous studies program at the University of Texas, for instance, is "particularly concerned with scholarship and intellectual exchange that contributes to the economic, social, and political advancement of indigenous peoples."[24] Likewise, American Indian studies at the University of Arizona, which explores "issues from American Indian perspectives which place the land, its history and the people at the center," makes clear its emphasis: "American Indian Studies promotes Indian self-determination, self-governance, and strong leadership as defined by Indian nations, tribes, and communities, all of which originated from the enduring beliefs and philosophies of our ancestors."[25] Similar professions of material engagement and commitment to self-determination are common. Such is the case in Palestine studies.

Interest in Palestine among Native scholars is logical. The field, after all, has long offered critique of U.S. empire and imperialism and produced comparative analyses of Indians with other racial and religious minorities. It is not surprising, then, that at least some attention be directed toward an expansionist Israel not only funded by the United States but claiming to be a modern incarnation and

proud conserver of American manifest destiny. Israel, we must remember, is often conceptualized by American elites and rank-and-
file Christians alike not merely as a worthy recipient of U.S.
patronage, but as an indivisible component of American cultural
identity. Barack Obama made clear this bond in his 2012 American
Israel Public Affairs Committee (AIPAC) speech: "The United States
and Israel share interests, but we also share those human values that
Shimon [Perez] spoke about: a commitment to human dignity. A
belief that freedom is a right that is given to all of God's children.
An experience that shows us that democracy is the one and only
form of government that can truly respond to the aspirations of
citizens."[26]

Yet there might be more to the growing importance of Palestine
to American Indian studies. I would suggest that interest in Palestine among Native and Indigenous scholars represents at least in
part a realization of the field's ideals of decolonial advocacy. I do
not raise this point to romanticize American Indian studies or to
totalize it. Rather, I suggest that any field with a commitment to
the repatriation of the communities it studies will eventually become
transnational because the powers against which the dispossessed
fight are interrelated. And because of a variety of phenomena, transnationalism in American Indian studies quickly moved to incorporate Palestine.

The comparison of the United States and Israel is particularly
germane around the concept of values, a term Obama emphasized
in his AIPAC speech. Less than a year after that speech, when former U.S. senator Chuck Hagel faced scrutiny as Obama's choice
as secretary of defense because of his supposed hostility to Israel
(an accusation with no basis in fact), Hagel responded to criticism
by proclaiming, "America's relationship with Israel is one that
is fundamentally built on our nations' shared values, common interests and democratic ideals."[27] Values, of course, are unstable
things—unreliable, too, because they are invested with so many
explicit and implicit demands and coercions. In this case, as Hagel's
passage indicates, there is a long-standing discourse of shared values between the United States and Israel that mutually implicates
Natives and Palestinians as premodern and unworthy of liberation.

What are those values? Democracy. Modernity. Industriousness. Freedom. Nobility. Humanity. Compassion. Natives and Palestinians not only lack these qualities, but actively seek to undermine them. American values arise not only from an expansionist capitalism but also from the redemptive mythologies of Israeli colonization, a fact that has led numerous people in American Indian studies to question the accuracy of Zionism's heroic narratives and to explore how the current situation of Palestinians under military occupation lends understanding to Native reinterpretations of those American values. As Kauanui notes,

> The politics of indigeneity bring much to bear on critical analyses of Israeli exceptionalism, as it is bolstered and bankrolled by an American exceptionalism that denies the colonization of Native North America. Comparative examinations of Israeli settler colonialism in relation to questions of occupation, self-determination and decolonization within the framework of international law demand ethical consideration by Native American and Indigenous Studies scholars.[28]

While the inclusion of Palestine in American Indian studies tells us much about the shifting possibilities of Palestine studies, particularly its uneasy relationship with Middle East studies, it also illuminates (or reinforces) a particular set of commitments in American Indian studies. Such is especially true of the material politics of decolonization and its role in the formation of certain liberationist ethics to which many practitioners of American Indian and Indigenous studies adhere. The analysis of Palestine in American Indian studies forces us to continue exploring the cultures and geographies of Indigeneity.

Here the issue of Palestine continues to prove instructive. In the culture wars of Israel–Palestine there is much chatter about the matter of Indigeneity. In fact, it is the central moral basis for claims of geographic and cultural ownership in the so-called Holy Land, a reality illuminated by former Canadian MP Irwin Cotler when he proclaimed, "Israel is the aboriginal homeland of the Jewish people across space and time. Its birth certificate originates in its inception as a First Nation, and not simply, however important, in its United Nations international birth certificate."[29] Cotler's claim is remarkable for numerous reasons. By appropriating the language of Indigenous peoplehood ("aboriginal," "First Nation"), Cotler positions Israel, against available historical evidence, as a presence dating to antiquity and a beneficiary of exceptional juridical standing based on a specific legal categorization.[30]

Although conceptually Cotler articulates a variant of the Zionist claim of Jewish ownership of Palestine, his language bespeaks an approach outside the commonplaces of Zionist discourse, which has largely focused on historical grievance (particularly European anti-Semitism), promissory narratives (God granted the land to Jews), and the inevitability of ingathering the diaspora (we were here in the past and thus have a right to be here in the present). In Cotler's argument, these commonplaces recede to assumptions as a new form of reasoning emerges, that of Israel as predecessor to the very existence of Palestinians, who become the conquerors, the foreigners, the aliens, the strangers. This argument rejects historical evidence of Palestinian dispossession and instead consigns them to the status of aggressor, stewards of their own suffering. Less obviously, it also disenfranchises Indigenous peoples in North America by subordinating their claims of nationhood into the logic of Western conquest. Cotler offers one example of the ability of Western multicultural practice to appropriate anything at its disposal in order to buttress an imperial power structure, for his pronouncement offers nothing to indicate that he would support a level of autonomy for Indigenous peoples in Canada similar to that enjoyed by the Israeli state.

Indeed, Zionists have consistently employed the language of Indigeneity—"*Jews* are indigenous to the land"—to explain the settlement of Palestine throughout the twentieth century or to rationalize the current settlement of the West Bank. Allen Z. Hertz, for instance, declares, "Conceptually, the Jewish people is aboriginal to its ancestral homeland in the same way that the First Nations are aboriginal to their ancestral lands in the Americas."[31] Palestinians in return often rely on the same language of Indigeneity to counter Zionist claims or to assert a moral narrative of belonging vis-à-vis the unjustness of foreign settlement. The New England

Committee to Defend Palestine describes the Israel–Palestine conflict as such: "It is a conflict between the indigenous Palestinian people and the Europeans who came with guns to steal their land and resources."[32] When Zionists and Palestinians lay claim to Indigeneity, they are not merely being technical. The term "Indigenous" is infused with numerous connotations about access, belonging, biology, culture, jurisdiction, and identity. Indigeneity is not simply a moral entitlement, but a legal and political category. To access that category is to be positioned as steward and legatee of a particular territory. Thus the appropriation of the language of Indians inherently recognizes Indians as the rightful indigenes of North America—a recognition made infrequently by politicians and commentators—and simultaneously appropriates Natives into an extraneous debate whose conduct invalidates their agency.

The debate invalidates Indian agency because rarely does it visualize Natives as living communities engaged in the work of repatriation—or even in the work of survival. When a person says "Jews are the Indians of the Holy Land," the statement affixes Indians into a specific historical posture that renders them rhetorical but not legal or contemporaneous claimants against colonization. This is so because the claim is fundamentally statist, referencing a particular history to support an argument of the present. The referenced history does not make it into the present. The argument it informs already occupies that space.

Further evidence that this sort of move invalidates Indian agency is available in the language of the rhetoric itself. One need only read major forums of debate—The *New York Times,* the *Washington Post, Slate*, the Huffington Post, and even social media such as Facebook and Twitter—to notice the extent to which visions of the American past bear upon the matter of Palestine. Attenuated notions of Indian dispossession frequently rationalize Palestinian dispossession. As Laila Al-Marayati observes, "Today, most Americans do not believe that the decimation and expulsion of entire Indian tribes in response to 'terrorist' attacks against wagon trains was justified. But, as one caller to a syndicated radio program suggested, since we're not about to give anything back to the Indians, why should the Israelis be expected to return stolen land to the Palestinians?"[33]

Unlike the Jews-as-Indians argument, this one acknowledges Indian disenfranchisement (again, only in the past), but excludes any possibility of repatriation. Yet, exactly like the Jews-as-Indians argument, the goal is to justify the original sins of Zionism and the current settlement of the West Bank. This time the Palestinians become Indians and both communities end up consigned to an unfortunate but inevitable antiquity overwhelmed by the progress of a linear history, another powerful example of how a colonial ethos allows people to own history without being responsible for it. The common wisdom and common sense of this argument arise from a settler logic of divine possession and democratic entitlement whose values—the hegemony of its assumptions—render conquest a permanent feature of modern American consciousness. Zionism has adopted this consciousness in its desire to normatize—that is, to render normative, as opposed to merely normal—garrison settlement and military occupation. For Zionists, colonization is permanent even as it happens—in many ways before it has even taken place, for the ideologies of modernity underlying expansionist worldviews emphasize the progress of a distinct state culture with a neoliberal economy and a militarized infrastructure. The idea of returning land to Indians is crazy, indeed, as crazy as the idea of allowing Palestinians to remain on theirs.

Ha'aretz columnist Ari Shavit offered an example of this phenomenon amid the debates inspired by his 2013 book *My Promised Land,* a compendium of settler dissimulation. In an interview with *New Yorker* editor David Remnick, Shavit professes his refusal to condemn the Israelis who participated in massacres of Palestinians in 1948. "Now I think it's very important to remember," he declares, "I mean, this country [the United States] is based on crimes that are much worse than Lydda, much worse than Lydda."[34] (The 1948 Israeli massacre in and depopulation of Lydda and the neighboring village of Ramle, which Shavit explores at length, resulted in the displacement of as many as seventy thousand Palestinians. Ben-Gurion International Airport sits atop the site of the two villages.) Remnick then asks Shavit about the difference between U.S. and Israeli massacres. "About a hundred years," Shavit replies.

Shavit avers that U.S. colonization is worse than its Israeli counterpart and implies that in the near future Zionist ethnic cleansing will matter less, in the same way that U.S. ethnic cleansing has been diminished by the passage of time. The implication likewise downplays the seriousness of Zionist ethnic cleansing in the present. I have negligible interest in the first claim, as I see little use in quantifying and then ranking mass suffering according to the peculiar algorithms of colonial guilt. The United States colonized hundreds of distinct nations; Israel colonized a handful, Palestine primarily. Shavit appears to be unaware of, or indifferent to, the multiplicity of conflicts and encounters in America, or of the ongoing struggles to decolonize the continent. Nor were Zionist massacres limited to Lydda and Ramle. There is nothing useful to say about Shavit's apocryphal one hundred–year gap between U.S. and Israeli colonization; we can merely highlight its spectacular wrongness.

His implications are worth notice, though. Time can only heal the past in specific circumstances—when the oppressive party makes amends, for example, or reverses destructive policies. For Shavit and like-minded commentators, though, time itself can progress beyond the resilience of memory. This conception of the world reinforces the temporal peculiarities of logic motivated by conquest and acquisition. The *nakba* matters less than the triumph of Zionism for no reason other than the triumph of American colonization. Shavit's argument, like those of similar interlocutors, is no more complex than this non sequitur. It imagines a permanent past because it cannot process complexities of the present. Shavit does not write history from the vantage point of the victor; he writes as a tenuous citizen anxious that victories of the past are only historical. The native, in other words, has not accepted the permanence of the colonizer. If Shavit were to acknowledge that Natives do not adhere to settler timelines, his arguments about Israeli timelessness would be impossible.

The Indian interventions into these debates are of special interest. Much of the scholarly and political opposition to Zionism moves beyond moral displeasure at the behavior of Israel and its American sponsor, concerning itself instead with broader questions of power and meaning. As Stephen P. Gasteyer and Cornelia Butler

Flora explain in their comparison of Palestine with Iowa and Patagonia, "the settlement of these areas involved processes of discovery, valuation, settlement, and conquest by outsiders. Part of the last two phases contained elements of equality but restricted equality to the dominant class, the conquerors (Jews in Palestine, later Israel, or European-Americans in the Patagonia and Iowa). Part of the conquest involved a rationale of taming, civilizing, and making more efficient a 'wild' land and 'savage' people."[35]

What, then, does it mean to confront a state whose presence, ipso facto, ensures legal and territorial dominance of its Indigenous communities and its legitimization as a permanent arbiter of its subjects' destinies? In the interrelated narratives of colonial permanence in the United States and Israel, we have a profound set of circumstances within which to explore this question. Answering the question from a perspective that does not take it as a point of fact that the United States and Israel are permanent has an added benefit of delegitimizing the state, but the primary function of the perspective is to imagine a future outside of the notion that displacement and disenfranchisement must be permanent simply because they succeeded.

I would emphasize that despite an abundance of American–Israeli interactions—military, economic, diplomatic, cultural, historical, religious—the relationship of the two states is most profound at a level of discourse and ideology. In fact, a manifest Holy Land ethos has played an enormous role in the development of American society, both physically and philosophically. As Tim Giago notes in highlighting the interconnectedness of Natives and Palestinians, "The early settlers believed it was God's will (Manifest Destiny) that the heathens be driven from the land. It was God's will that the land be settled and populated by white Christians. They looked upon the indigenous population as a mere obstacle to be slaughtered or removed."[36] That ethos predates the creation of Israel, but also presupposes it. In this sense, the ancient Israel of the Old Testament was realized not through modern Zionism but in the settlement of North America.

Steven Newcomb explores these phenomena in his book *Pagans in the Promised Land*. He notes that "when dominating forms of reasoning (categorization) found in the Old Testament narrative are unconsciously used to reason about American Indians, Indian lands metaphorically become—from the viewpoint of the United States—the promised land of the chosen people of the United States."[37] Newcomb's analysis is valuable, though I would question the extent to which reasoning about American Indians as biblical Canaanites is unconscious. The teleology of North America as a new promised land is obvious in the early days of European settlement, but even now the inventions of America as a metaphorical Israel, with Indians as a romanticized but ungodly presence, remains common—quite consciously so.

These discursive geographies have traveled continuously between North America and Palestine. In turn, the geographies of American Indian and Indigenous studies have transcended the restrictions inherent to the nation-state, the quintessential entity of colonization. In so doing, the field challenges the probity of the nation-state as a governing authority and progenitor of social organization. As Duane Champagne notes in the introduction to a comparative collection coedited with Palestinian Ismael Abu-Saad examining the future of Indigenous peoples, "Native struggles within nation-state systems are not simply efforts to gain inclusion or access to citizenship. . . . Native peoples wish to preserve land, economic subsistence and means, and political and cultural autonomy. In many cases, nation-states often find the demands of Native communities threatening, at odds with national policies of integration and assimilation."[38]

This passage illuminates one of the central features of inter/national scholarship, its insistence on transnational dialogue extraneous and opposed to the physical and legal parameters of the nation-state.

Performing Inter/Nationalism

In closing, I would like to offer a few thoughts about the conditions of performing inter/nationalist scholarship.

In many ways, Palestine has become a test case of one's bona fides in American studies, ethnic studies, and other areas of inquiry—

likewise in political and community organizations beyond academe. To be opposed to, say, the Iraq invasion while simultaneously supporting Israel ensures, at least among a considerable demographic, a loss or weakening of credibility. Anti-Zionism as test case of one's trustworthiness represents the ascension of Palestine into the consciousness of the political and academic Left and, more important, into the worldwide collective of Indigenous scholars challenging the structures and mores of academic convention. This ascension of Palestine arises from the recognition, always evident but now common, that Israel is not merely an ally or client of the United States, but a profound component of its imperial practice. To support Israel is to support U.S. empire; thus other professions of resistance to U.S. empire come into conflict with their own values in the presence of Zionism.

Any political or methodological commitment as a litmus test is inherently problematic, for the litmus test can render struggle a fashion responsive to the recital of slogans or coded professions of support. Palestine can become a thin signifier of interpersonal belonging rather than a site of serious reckoning vis-à-vis the multidisciplinary spaces that accommodate its presence. Those inherent problems notwithstanding, the juxtaposition of Natives and Palestinians represents a deterritorialization of traditional disciplinary areas. In many ways, it makes more sense for Palestine studies and Indigenous studies to be in conversation than Palestine studies and Middle East studies, as Middle East studies encompasses vast geographies in which liberation of Palestine is but a specialized subset and has traditionally accommodated various incarnations of Zionism as well as institutional acceptance of Israel, in its current ethnocentric form, as a permanent reality.

For scholars serious about better comprehending Palestine's present and working to ensure its future, American Indian studies offers more groundbreaking and germane critique than do the Cold War–era area studies. In Palestine, American Indian studies participants can access a view of history as it has been reinvented in the present, wherein the residue of conquest continues in North America through plutocratic governance and functions in Palestine through the old-fashioned use of soldiers, tanks, tear gas, guns, grenades, and armed settlers, a violent continuation of the U.S. legacy of Holy Land mythmaking and ostensible reclamation.

Conducting this type of work on campus presents challenges, some of them irreconcilable with the ethical commonplaces of American Indian studies. We do much of our teaching and research on public space, in the case of those who work in state institutions, so immediately the task of decolonization extends to the very site of our sustenance. The task of American Indian studies, then, involves constant attention to the seemingly benign iterations of land theft and dispossession. Adding Palestine to the mix intensifies the task, but to our enrichment, and, importantly, to the detriment of those invested in the colonial university.

2.
BOYCOTTING ISRAEL AS NATIVE NATIONALISM

■   ■   ■

On December 4, 2013, the American Studies Association (ASA) adopted a resolution pledging to honor the academic boycott of Israel. The resolution passed after the ASA National Council, which is vested with decision-making authority, took the unusual step of requesting a vote from the membership at large. The council had unanimously approved the resolution, but felt it prudent to also hold an election, one in which 68 percent of respondents voted in the affirmative (with a considerably higher participation rate than the average ASA election).

The resolution inspired widespread discussion within and outside the United States, and far beyond academic circles. The *Chronicle of Higher Education* devoted considerable space to the resolution (and to academic boycott more broadly). Major papers such as the *New York Times,* the *Washington Post, Ha'aretz,* the *Wall Street Journal,* and the *Los Angeles Times* ran both news and opinion pieces about the ASA. BDS was suddenly a major topic of conversation in popular discourse. It proved to be highly unpopular among corporate media and campus administrators. More than one hundred university presidents and provosts released statements condemning the ASA for supposed violations of academic freedom or scholarly decorum. Three states—Illinois, New York, and Maryland—have considered legislation that would defund individuals or departments who hold ASA membership. As of this writing, more legislative bodies, including the U.S. Congress, are considering similar action. The venerable academic freedom watchdog group, the American Association of University Professors (AAUP), strongly condemned the ASA and rejected academic boycotts on principle (a stance that does not fully cohere with the organization's partial support of the academic boycott of South African institutions during apartheid).

More pointed forms of resistance arose. ASA leaders and members of its Community and Activism Caucus, which had sponsored the resolution, were subject to considerable online harassment, including death threats and the release of private information. Angry ideologues flooded the ASA Facebook page with a litany of racist and sexist comments. Michael Oren, the former Israeli ambassador to the United States, accused then-ASA president Curtis Marez of anti-Semitism in an essay at *Politico*. Israeli Prime Minister Benjamin Netanyahu inveighed against BDS at the 2014 American Israel Public Affairs Committee (AIPAC) conference, declaring, "BDS is morally wrong."[1]

In this chapter, I explore the implications of academic boycott in the context of broader questions about decolonization, emphasizing the geographies of Indigeneity in America. While issues of academic freedom and activist strategy are central to BDS, it is important to keep sight of the movement's engagement with the landscapes from which it arises. "Landscapes" references both dialogue and the actual land that defines Indigenous cultures. What does it mean for a BDS movement, one originating in Palestine, to do work in America, itself a colonized space? In what ways can and should BDS interact with Native communities? How do Native communities inform the tactics and philosophies of BDS? I will argue that BDS actually functions as an articulation of Native sovereignty, inside and beyond America, but only when it transcends its own nationalist paradigms. I propose we measure the success of BDS by how effectively it undermines American state power in addition to the militant colonialism of its Israeli client.

What Is Academic Boycott?

It might be useful to offer some history of academic boycott before proceeding. It is by no means a simple history, for while the academic boycott of Israel has a discernible origin, academic boycott itself precedes focus on Israeli institutions. Also complicating matters are the informal boycotts of many varieties directed against Israel in the Arab world, in addition to state-sanctioned embargoes, many of which have dissipated because of legal and diplomatic pressure by the United States.

Decades before the ASA's infamous resolution, academic boycott of South African institutions had achieved international prominence. I do not intend to recount the antiapartheid boycott movement beyond noting that, while different in important ways from BDS in both strategy and context, it has had a serious influence on the discourses and organizational practices of today's scholar-activists.[2] Proponents of the ASA resolution often invoke the academic boycott of South Africa as a moral example and historical precedent.[3] The boycott of Israeli universities, then, rehearses histories intrinsic to and external of its own subjectivity.

Political and economic boycotts of Israel at the level of state are less germane, but nevertheless relevant. The refusal to maintain diplomatic relations with Israel can be seen as a form of boycott, but one that arises from the specificities of national governance, an arena in which the United States Academic and Cultural Boycott of Israel (USACBI) (likewise its parent group, Palestinian Academic and Cultural Boycott of Israel [PACBI]) is pointedly uninterested. These broader interactions with Israel may not significantly affect PACBI or USACBI's work, but they still inform the history of BDS. Many Arab- and Muslim-majority nations have no formal ties with Israel, but maintain informal relations, either as oligarchs in business ventures or through secret channels of cooperation. State actors cannot be removed from the inveterate spectacle of the ulterior motive. An effective boycott of Israel, then — one trained on just outcomes and not on realpolitik or profit — must necessarily retain a grassroots character, even after it ceases to be marginal.

For these reasons, remaining independent of state support has been critical to BDS activists for practical in addition to philosophical reasons. Diplomatic boycotts have circulated ideas and enacted political values, but they have not been effective in mobilizing against colonization. In fact, plenty of evidence suggests that mobilization is actively suppressed by the same governments that nominally boycott Israel.[4] Although BDS targets Israeli institutions, it does not treat Israel as exceptional, leading sometimes to systemic condemnation that includes Arab and Western governments. BDS is not symbiotic with the boycotts of Israel that predate it. Rather, it sustains a productive tension with the past that presupposes contemporary moral and tactical analysis.

It is also useful to situate academic boycott within the history of Palestine activism in North America, Europe, and the Arab world. That history is too extensive and complex to adequately synthesize, but it helps us understand the coalescence of BDS into a distinctive, organized movement. Arab communities—sometimes deemed "civil society" in boycott parlance—have long practiced various types of boycott against Israel. Diasporic Palestinians (and other Arab and Muslim groups) have for decades refused to buy Israeli products in European and American markets. Rejecting engagement with individuals and institutions tied to Israeli state funding has been a de facto practice if not an actual policy. The concept of boycotting Israel, then, is not new; it has been a feature of Arab nationalist politics since before Israel's creation. BDS differs from these predecessors (and contemporaries) in both organization and praxis, but it is useful to recall that PACBI has not generated a movement from scratch (nor does it make that sort of claim). While boycotts of apartheid states were formalized long before BDS constituted itself around a specific set of principles, boycotts of Israel occurred simultaneous to those of Rhodesia and South Africa.[5]

Academic boycott is not a static practice and entails constant internal dialogue (I serve on the USACBI organizing committee), but we can ultimately measure it as a form of rejectionism, putting it into conversation with the broader traditions from which it emerged. By "rejectionism," I do not mean reflexive anti-Zionism (though it can be accommodated by the term), but a rejection of détente as a diplomatic maneuver at the level of state. Encompassed in this form of rejection are ethical repudiations of neocolonial and neoliberal models of conflict resolution, those sponsored by states and international bodies like the United Nations. Rejection likewise encompasses wariness (and weariness) of tactics and commitments dictated by voices from the colonial society. Finally, the term aims to reject conventional deceits of modernity, in which insurgency is necessarily subsumed to the prerogatives of the state. In total, then, rejectionism is the common base of BDS because the structures of colonial power do not allow dissent beyond carefully managed principles repeatedly consumed by their own liberal discourses.

The terminologies of the acronym BDS—boycott, divestment, sanctions—illuminate important features of its history. Movements in America to sanction and divest from Israel precede academic and cultural boycott (at least in its formal incarnation), but they also form something of a continuum to the ethics and tactics of those asking scholarly organizations to endorse USACBI's call for solidarity. Beyond rejectionism, that continuum includes the prevalence of college campuses as sites of action, emphasis on the necessity of Palestinian voices, and disengagement from the orthodoxies of liberal Zionism (dialogue, coexistence, soul-searching, ethnocentrism, identification with state security apparatuses, and so forth). Despite its origin in the Arab world, academic boycott of Israel, as taken up in America, can be seen as an evolution of divestment and sanctions into a comprehensive grassroots movement. Sanction and divestiture are both forms of boycott—at least if read broadly—and so BDS is not necessarily an amalgamation. It might be better described as a culmination.

The principles of BDS are not stagnant (and have evolved from its point of inception), but academic boycott operates with a set of basic practices and assumptions, which have coalesced in part because of its adoption into wider practice. The structure of USACBI is of interest because, as with any organization, it illuminates its central values. (Indeed, it is useful to discern values through assessment of praxis rather than acceptance of mission statements.) USACBI's structure is difficult to synthesize because it is amorphous by design. If anything, the organization abides by certain tenets of anarchism in that it eschews top-down authority and has no officers. While it has informal arrangements of power and members with different levels of influence, no constitutional hierarchy exists. We reach decisions through consensus, defined in our case by a preponderance of agreement with no vocalized opposition. If a member disapproves of a proposed action, discussion ensues; if the dissenting member does not stand down from his or her disapproval, then the conversation continues. Without an adequate resolution, the action stalls, unless the dissenter approves of its adoption while maintaining his or her disagreement. Student members of the organizing committee (OC) have the same formal power as senior professors.

This arrangement might seem cumbersome, but in reality it is fluid and has proved remarkably efficient. Serious disagreement rarely occurs, and when it does, reasoned discussion effectively ameliorates it. The size of the organizing committee might have something to do with this efficiency, another counterintuitive possibility belied by actualities of nonhierarchical cooperation. A large organizing committee—thirty-five members at the time of this writing—allows individuals to drop in and out of activity without affecting the work of the group as a whole. Some OC members are consistently active, while others focus on specific issues. Still others only contribute occasionally. Yet everybody's consent or dissent is weighted equally. My point is not to romanticize the OC, but to identify an actively democratic organizing structure that coheres to the philosophy of our work. This cohesion is relevant insofar as it enables BDS to be performative rather than utilitarian. The OC, then, exists in stark opposition to the groups working against BDS. Such groups are well funded by outside interests and are deeply invested in state institutions as a form of grievance and redress, or, in many cases, as a means to marginalize or criminalize dissent.

That groups working against BDS are funded by lobbyists and governments is crucial to our understanding of the ethical imperatives of Palestine activists.[6] USACBI and the BDS movement more generally attach to larger issues of neoliberalism, contingent labor, institutional racism, Native treaty rights, global decolonization, corporatized education, and academic freedom. These interactions result from both the inherent priorities of BDS and conscious out-reach. I would welcome further emphasis on and engagement with issues (seemingly) beyond BDS's immediate orbit. As I argue later in this chapter, BDS has a particular responsibility to American decolonization. In fact, it emerges from an inter/national context, making America impossible to disregard even if it is ignored. (It is not, though I believe America needs to be more central to BDS work.) In any case, as a campaign purporting to influence a geopolitical outcome, BDS activism requires engagement with numerous modes of state and plutocratic domination. Zionist commitments are concordant with, and constitutive of, the many pressure points affecting the vulnerable and powerless.

As to the practices and assumptions of USACBI, these are my impressions of the OC as both an observer and a participant.

Central practices:

- Nonhierarchical

- Consensus-based

- Self-funded

- Unaffiliated

- Nondenominational

- No formal position on one- versus two-state solution

- Antiauthoritarian

- Collaborative

- Independent

The OC is also governed by shared assumptions, some of which are actual policies, while others arise from common preferences without constituting dicta or injunctions.

- Palestinians are afforded priority in disseminating the OC's narratives. For example, I, of Palestinian origin on my maternal side, was encouraged to be part of the media team during the process to pass the ASA resolution. At the level of policy, Palestinians are not offered a distinctive positionality per se, but their opinions carry a special weight, even if that weight provides no formal authority, but rather influences the mechanisms of developing consensus.

- We do not evoke state institutions (courts, law enforcement, legislatures) as a remedy to injustice, but treat those institutions as impediments to the pursuit of justice.

- PACBI, as the Arabic-language and Palestine-based collective, sets policy around boycott criteria and the governance of various actions. The USACBI OC contributes to the process through consistent interchange, but more or less works autonomously on various American projects.

- We make no firm distinction between 1948 and 1967 Israel (i.e., Israel inside the Green Line versus the Occupied Territories). The indisputable evidence of Israeli discrimination against its Palestinian citizens is integral to our use of boycott as an instrument of justice.[7] USACBI supports multiple sectors of Palestinian society.

- The right of return for Palestinian refugees is central to USACBI's program. Israel's repudiation of international law vis-à-vis the population it displaced is a vital reason BDS exists. Israel's unwillingness to entertain a return of refugees has precipitated emphasis on grassroots pressure and public awareness, both inherent to BDS.

- The OC has no formal—or, as far as I know, informal— relationships with governments or political parties. We receive no input from the Palestinian Authority or Hamas, nor do we engage institutions representing the American or Israeli states. We only deal with nongovernmental organizations (NGOs) insofar as they express a willingness to endorse BDS.

By late 2013, BDS had emerged as the most visible feature of Palestine solidarity activism. There has been considerable discussion of the tactic in addition to the Israeli practices it condemns. In particular, advocates and opponents of BDS have explored its efficacy in relation to its stated goals (with the opponents often charging BDS activists with deception—that is, working toward more nefarious ends than they state publicly).[8]

It is worth undertaking systematic assessment of BDS efficacy, something we can do by assessing its purposes and outcomes.

In terms of its purposes, BDS attempts numerous things simultaneously, all interconnected. It aims to condemn the behavior of the Israeli state, but also to affect material conditions in Palestine. It is also invested in the conditions of discursive practice around the world vis-à-vis Israeli colonization. In North America, for example, the balance has long tilted toward pro-Israel narratives; BDS advocates in the United States and Canada, then, attempt to alter the commonplaces of this reality. "Material conditions" include state violence, economic disenfranchisement, political marginalization, and legal discrimination. The ultimate goal of BDS is to mitigate, and preferably to end, those material conditions and secure basic rights of self-determination for the Palestinians (e.g., to return, to reside, to participate, and to belong). BDS has never existed solely in moral or philosophical tableaus. It purports to do more than persuade or condemn. Its ultimate goals are concordant with the aspirations of Palestine's national movement. Those goals do not include "the destruction of Israel," as the oft-repeated meme has it, nor does it target Jews as ethnoreligious communities, as some have claimed.[9] They do, however, include restitution and redress for the Palestinian people, which are, according to poor ideological logic, incompatible with Jewish freedom—in reality the logic bespeaks incompatibility with the cultural and biological strictures of Zionism.

Those against academic boycott, both on and off campus, consistently invoke academic freedom as the reason for their position (though some confess loyalty to Zionism as a motivation).[10] A boycott, the argument goes, would restrict the academic freedom of Israeli scholars and impinge on the exchange of ideas so crucial to scholarly life. This assertion has consistently been unmasked as fallacious.[11] Academic boycott is careful to distinguish between institutions and individuals. Some have observed that the distinction is functionally impossible, but only individuals who consciously participate in advocacy for the Israeli state would be affected.[12] Boycott transfers responsibility to the individual, but never targets her for preemptive exclusion. In this sense, academic boycott is consummately reactive.

Academic boycott does not systematically limit an Israeli scholar's ability to travel and conduct research. (In fact, the ASA has formally hosted Israeli citizens on numerous occasions.) On the other hand, engagement with Palestine has repeatedly proved deleterious to one's professional development. It has long been a truism among academics that speaking in support of Palestine is an excellent way to forestall tenure or promotion. Some scholars have been fired for such support, and dozens have been incessantly harassed and subjected to campaigns for their termination. The question of academic freedom, then, should be trained on those who have been punished for speech or advocacy. It is usually directed at those in the camp of the oppressor, instead. Academic boycott never acts on a person's expression of views, but on his actions. Does he perform at the behest of the government of Israel? If so, he is actively participating in the subjugation of Palestinian students and scholars and thus subject to boycott.

In short, boycott is not a contravention of academic freedom, but an expression of it.

The tactics of those opposed to boycott affirm the importance of the movement. Beyond the turn to government elites and university presidents, a strategy I call "the appeal to authority," many states have introduced legislation that aims to defund departments whose memberships have any ties to the ASA. The appeal to authority is reliant on the cultural and political elite and on legislative bodies to offer a corrective to grassroots agitating. While BDS continues to generate support among students, activists, and performers, the opposition cultivates patronage from centers of power: university presidents, politicians, state senates, financiers, and so forth. This difference is important: it shows the juxtaposition of Zionism with violent conduct while USACBI has successfully avoided the coercions of sectarian loyalty. Organizations that maintain dossiers on pro-Palestine activists and work closely with surveillance agencies to suppress dissent really have no choice but to evoke the repressive apparatuses of state power in order to counter threats to their supremacy.

In my opinion, the greatest strength of BDS is its desire to remain adamantly independent, accepting cues from Palestinian civil society, because movements for justice work well only in proportion to their freedom from vested interests. Activism should always inform a multivalent radius based on an antagonistic relationship with sources of political and economic power. The ethical distinctions between BDS activists and our opponents are discernible relative to the affinities each camp maintains with institutions that rely on laws and guns to enforce compliance. USACBI does not need the endorsement of university presidents or lawmaking bodies. Nor does it *want* their endorsement, which would constitute an abdication of what BDS works to accomplish, decolonization of the institutions those bodies exist to enrich and represent. The appeal to authority constitutes a serious form of oppositional force. It will exist as long as Zionism remains synchronous to the neoliberal order. However, the appeal to authority is not a threat to USACBI. It is a validation of both the structure and the content of our work.

Academic boycott, therefore, enters into spaces that dictate how we conduct ourselves as scholars. It likewise amplifies ethical questions about the function of the scholar within her own milieu as well as in public sites of debate. Does the scholar have a material or moral obligation to the communities he studies or that influence his research? Is the scholar's duty merely to observe and analyze the world, or should he participate in the geographies of his observation and analysis? Is it part of a scholar's purview to agitate for more just policies or against unjust practice outside her place of employment? If so, what ethical and pragmatic considerations limit her agitation?

In examining these questions, it is a good idea to discard absolutes such as "duty," "obligation," and "responsibility." They are fundamentally inflexible, but also can render dissent mechanical and unilateral. The questions have some automatic answers: scholars already participate in the geographies of their observation and analysis whether or not they acknowledge that reality. Scholars who do not agitate for justice, or at least against injustice, have already made a deliberate choice to politicize academe. The ethical and pragmatic considerations that should limit a scholar's desire to agitate depend on the purpose and target of the agitation. It is wise to keep in mind that it is quite difficult to find forms of neoliberal oppression in which U.S. (and international) universities are not somehow complicit. As a result, commitment to material, rather than merely intellectual, outcomes is usually necessary, or at least justifiable. The greater question is whether or not scholars should agitate outside their places of employment. Here is where ethical and pragmatic considerations prevail. There is much to debate, but my foremost conclusion is that our places of employment already create significant agitation in the world, so they inevitably bind us to the geopolitics they influence. Scholars exist in the same world as everybody else, even when they pretend to transcend and illuminate it. Dislodging academics from the fantasies of disinterested observation renders the matter of agitation starker, which offers better moral clarity.

It is useful to explore the questions I raise above in the context of a dynamic view of scholarly labor. Appeals to responsibility do not generally illuminate the complex interchanges of activism and scholarship. I am loath to demand, ipso facto, any form of advocacy, but the real stakes do not exist in the framework of individual agency; they exist in structural impositions of institutional conformity. In many ways, the decision to become active in issues beyond one's university (if such a possibility even exists) depends not on the individual but on the implicit conditions of employment. (Sometimes those conditions are explicit.) What is the institutional culture around outspoken faculty? Do administrators tend to deny tenure and promotion to provocative or insouciant professors? How tolerant are individual departments of unorthodox pedagogies and political commitments? These questions are central to the practice of academic boycott, which is not best described as extracurricular.

When we choose to practice academic boycott, then, we simultaneously reveal important facets of our research, service, pedagogy, and outreach. It is one way of claiming investment in material praxis as a form of analysis and observation. Universities have never been especially accommodating of dissent, and have been downright hostile to dissent that challenges state power, so academic boycott is deeply troublesome to administrators and a broad cross section of faculty (not limited to the humanities and social sciences, but mostly concentrated there). One cannot endorse academic boycott without also implicitly staking a position on questions of faculty engagement. For this reason, it is important to couch boycott in an analysis of various unjust campus practices, from exploited labor to militarism to inadequate protection against sexual assault and racism. We can develop relevant connections accordingly, in both pragmatic and philosophical capacities. Concerns around the leveraging of institutional power on the individual subject will always prevail in the presence of heterodoxy. When institutional power flexes itself around academic boycott, it is immaterial insofar as the circumstances of influence in academe tie into monetized incentives in which USACBI has no interest beyond their connections to Israel's occupation and the attendant elements of American complicity.

The outcomes of BDS praxis have been predictable, with some distinct surprises. Everybody in USACBI and in ASA leadership positions knew there would be pushback when it became clear the boycott resolution was a serious possibility (I speak here of external pushback; I examine pushback from within the ASA later in this chapter). The Association for Asian American Studies (AAAS) had approved a similar resolution six months prior, resulting in considerable acrimony.[13] Other organizations, too, have found their choices widely debated in both North America and Europe. Clearly, an ASA boycott of Israeli universities would generate similar attention. In fact, inevitable controversy was part of the conversation about the wisdom or stupidity of a boycott resolution. The intensity of the response, however, was remarkable. The ASA, heretofore a midsize scholarly association little known beyond academe, immediately found itself an exemplar of everything contentious in debates about the Israel–Palestine conflict.

The ASA's Facebook page filled with comments from indignant and enraged visitors. Then-president Curtis Marez and then-president-elect Lisa Duggan both received death threats. Major media in the United States, Canada, Europe, Israel, the Arab world, Latin America, and South Asia covered and editorialized about the resolution. The *Chronicle of Higher Education,* the flagship publication of academe, ran a series of articles and comments. Whereas the AAAS resolution resulted in outrage among pro-Israel advocacy organizations, the ASA resolution momentarily entered into the zeitgeist.

Many have explored what that sort of debate and publicity achieves. If the ultimate goal of BDS is a just resolution to the Israel–Palestine conflict, it will require much more than newspaper coverage. It is important to distinguish between the affairs of state power and the conduct of discourse in public spheres, but the two phenomena nevertheless influence one another. For this reason, I am optimistic that BDS has the potential to contribute to a broader global struggle, on multiple fronts, that might one day produce a positive outcome for Palestinians. Challenging any form of oppression is necessarily a multivalent commitment. The ASA resolution, then, is not merely symbolic, even if it might be a stretch to call it authoritative.

My observation is that the resolution performed crucial discursive work. Supporters of Israel found themselves in a defensive position, made to rationalize policies that usually inhabit a normative status (preferential immigration laws for Jews, lack of democratic access for Palestinian citizens of Israel, the importance of maintaining a Jewish demographic majority). Prominent liberals in particular were forced to answer to the inherent contradictions of Zionism. Peter Beinart, for example, wrote:

> The best argument against the ASA's boycott isn't about double standards or academic freedom. It's about the outcome the boycott seeks to produce. The Association's boycott resolution doesn't denounce "the Israeli occupation of the West Bank." It denounces "the Israeli occupation of Palestine" and "the systematic discrimination against Palestinians," while making no distinction whatsoever between Israeli control of the West Bank, where Palestinians lack citizenship, the right to vote and

the right to due process, and Israel proper, where Palestinians, although discriminated against, enjoy all three.[14]

Beinart also decries the resolution's presumptive desire to counter "Israel's right to maintain the preferential immigration policy that makes it a refuge for Jews." Here Beinart, as elsewhere, admits the he opposes BDS because he supports retention of Israel's ethnocratic character.[15] Nowhere is this fact more clearly articulated than in the phrase "although discriminated against," referring to Palestinian Israelis.

With the phrase, Beinart waves away discrimination as a trifling inconvenience. Yet the discrimination he passingly references is the heart of the matter, not an inconvenience to be acknowledged and then promptly ignored. BDS targets Israel in addition to the Occupied Territories precisely because of the discrimination to which Beinart accedes. The boycott does not make the distinction Beinart would like to see because the same state that pulverizes democracy on the West Bank makes a mockery of democracy inside Israel. There is no such thing as real democracy in legal systems that create hierarchies of access and belonging based on nothing more than biology. This is exactly the sort of troublesome feature of liberal Zionism that often went unchallenged until BDS earned prominence. After the ASA resolution, liberal Zionists needed to make that argument explicit in order to counter their opponents' moral petitions. Pragmatism is an excellent antidote to inconvenient facts. The best reason to oppose BDS, Beinart and others suggest, is that it threatens Israel's legal practice of eugenics. If anything, the ASA resolution made the debate more honest.

Another outcome of the resolution is the renewed attention on Palestine. That attention was helped by the fact of yet another failed peace process, this one eliciting widespread derision as it occurred and therefore highlighting BDS as an alternative to diplomacy. Because academic boycott targets Israel, it often compels observers to investigate, or at least to confront, the set of issues by which it is justified. In turn, boycott has further entrenched Palestine as a matter of great import on both the academic and the political left (which are not necessarily coterminous). BDS constitutes various discourses through which much conversation about and condemnation of Israel occurs.

If I can be permitted to reduce a complex phenomenon to a declaration: Palestine is no longer, and will likely not again become, a marginal issue.

Myths and Realities of BDS

It's instructive to think of BDS in relation to similar boycott movements, both contemporaneous and in the past. Few people these days would argue that the boycott of apartheid South Africa was counterproductive, unethical, ineffective, disingenuous, or unfair to the white minority. Likewise, when calls were issued to boycott Arizona in the aftermath of its legislation that demanded the profiling of Latino/as (and, implicitly, other people of color) in 2012, I saw nowhere near the same level of concern or hesitation as that generated by Palestinian BDS in the conversation among scholars. Indeed, much more stodgy and conventional associations than ASA refused to hold conferences in Arizona for years when the state would not recognize Martin Luther King Jr. Day.

My observation is that boycotts in themselves are not especially controversial among academic communities. In other words, BDS is not controversial. *Criticism of Israel* is controversial.

Even those who opposed boycott of South Africa or Arizona understood that white folks were not the victims of inequitable economies and legal systems. What sets Palestine apart is the persistent notion that the colonizers, those with nuclear weapons and land and resources and legislative power and the full support of the United States, are the oppressed party, that they largely suffer the pain and indignity of the conflict, that BDS is furtively anti-Semitic, that Israel is a special case in history, that it is distasteful to single out Israel. Remove this insidious reasoning and most rationalizations for rejecting boycott go away.

Here are the facts: no evidence has ever been presented that the Israeli government is interested in a viable solution to the conflict. Instead, Israel has persistently built illegal settlements, intensified its Judaization programs, shot and arrested children, appropriated land, destroyed olive groves, flouted international law, funded reactionary counterrevolutions, and passed overtly racist legislation, all of it with indisputable, institutional participation from Israeli universities.

More facts: the people of Palestine have been subject to a project of settler colonization for nearly 150 years, a period as long as the French occupation of Algeria. More than a million Palestinians live in refugee camps throughout the Arab world, many in severe poverty. Palestinian citizens of Israel inhabit the lower level of a two-tiered legal system that limits their rights to employment, land ownership, education, mobility, free expression, political participation, and public services. The Gaza Strip is destitute and overcrowded, victim of an ongoing Israeli campaign to strangle its economy with the express purpose of making its residents starve and suffer. The West Bank is carved into hundreds of inaccessible geographies separated by segregated highways, settlements, checkpoints, military instillations, and concrete walls.

Despite these horrible realities, this antediluvian system of biological determinism, we are told repeatedly by those opposed to BDS that the desires of the colonizer supersede the rights of the colonized. They rarely put it that way, but it is the primary assumption underlying the mistaken argument that BDS harms innocent Israelis, or is unfair to Israeli academics, or only makes the conflict worse. By this logic, the black boycott of Montgomery's bus system would have been unjustified because it might have harmed the drivers.

The most innocuous-sounding but insidious of these colonial apologetics assails us about the need for dialogue, not rejectionism. Yet BDS is not merely a tactic born of ahistorical circumstances. It is a movement for justice that has arisen from a need for action as a result of failures of dialogue over multiple decades, a dialogue utterly dominated by Zionist voices. Besides, I would argue that BDS constitutes a form of dialogue, one in which the Palestinian people are finally able to participate. Their contribution to this new dialogue is the announcement that they will never tolerate dispossession and will never accept their fate as expendable in the Zionist narrative.

Finally, Palestinians have not asked for dialogue as a form of solidarity. Nor have they—remarkably, considering the circumstances—asked anybody to shun others based on ethnicity or religion. What they have asked for is quite simple: that we honor their request to avoid validating, supporting, or engaging Israel's profound colonial apparatus, of which the state's universities are part and parcel.

I want to address the major myths about BDS and offer some correctives.

Myth: BDS constitutes a ban on Israelis.

Reality: Bans and boycotts are separate phenomena. The boycott neither acts as a ban in itself nor proposes to ban Israelis or anybody else from conducting their professional or personal business. Certain products are banned under BDS, but not people. The people who would be banned under BDS act as representatives of Israeli institutions by purporting to speak on behalf of those institutions or by acting as an emissary of institutional authority. Even then, the term "ban" does not accommodate the nuance of BDS principles.

Myth: The boycott of Israeli universities impinges on academic freedom.

Reality: We need to be clear: *Israel's occupation* impinges on academic freedom, that of all Palestinians and the Jews who dissent against national mythologies. For supporters of Israel to argue on the basis of academic freedom vis-à-vis boycott is more than bad irony; it is a hypocrisy of dreadful proportions. One of the goals of academic boycott is to undermine the informal embargo in universities against criticism of Israel. That informal embargo exists because for decades running afoul of the acceptable boundaries of critique enacted by Zionists resulted in all kinds of career impediments, including termination. Many of those complaining about restricted academic freedom for Israelis would do well to direct their concern toward actual victims of restriction, scholars harmed by the very system the ones complaining aim to maintain.

More important, in Palestine limits on academic freedom are brutally enforced. Israel repeatedly shuts down universities, sometimes for months at a time, compelling professors to hold impromptu classes in their living rooms. Checkpoints and other persistent restrictions on movement make it difficult for Palestinian faculty, students, and employees to arrive on campus, or to return home. The embargo on traveling between Gaza and the West Bank means that, for decades, students from Gaza have studied illegally on the West Bank. Palestinian students are arrested without charge or trial. The poverty engendered by military occupation makes access to education a difficult proposition. Speaking on controversial matters can land one in an Israeli court. The list goes on.

Academic boycott works to end these violations of both professional ethics and human rights.

Even if they actually existed, and they do not, the violations of academic freedom falsely imagined of boycott would be miniscule compared to the very real repression of academic freedom both Palestinians and their supporters in the United States must constantly navigate.

Myth: Israeli academe has nothing to do with the occupation.

Reality: Israeli universities, nearly all operated by the state, have been implicated in the development of weapons systems for the IDF, logistical analyses of settlement expansion, surveillance technologies, military training, cultivation of stolen land, and improving communications devices to be used in suppressing nonviolent protest. These are all forms of material complicity. Israeli universities also provide platforms from which the state can maintain its ideological apparatuses.

Myth: Targeting Israeli academe is foolish because it is filled with liberals who are natural allies of the Palestinians.

Reality: Haifa University graduate student Teddy Katz was put on trial for writing a master's thesis on the 1948 Israeli massacre of Palestinian civilians at Tantura. Neve Gordon was nearly fired from Ben-Gurion University of the Negev for advocating BDS. Ilan Pappe was driven from Israel because of his support of Palestinians. Israel's Council of Higher Education tried to shut down the entire department of politics at Ben-Gurion University. Even if individual progressive academics could save Palestine—and they cannot, and will never be able to—the idea of forestalling boycott to accommodate their righteousness is untenable. If Israeli academics wish to join the boycott in order to express their dissent, they are welcome in the movement. Plenty of Israeli academics already endorse BDS.

Myth: BDS is anti-Semitic.

Reality: This assertion rests on the idea that BDS targets Jews, which is empirically untrue. BDS targets Israeli corporations and institutions. It can only be called anti-Semitic if we accept the notion that Israeli institutions embody all Jewish people. And if we accept that notion, then we must also accept the notion that Jewish culture is inherently violent.

Myth: BDS unfairly singles out Israel.

Reality: BDS does not single out any one state or institution. It responds to a call from Palestinian civil society to adhere to a boycott based on a specific set of oppressive practices. It is also accordant with a number of contemporary and historical boycotts, Apartheid South Africa in particular. To say, in response to the identification of an injustice, "other people do it, too," does not absolve one of that injustice.

In fact, BDS aims to *end* the singling out of Israel. No nation engages in such terrible abuses of human rights with so much U.S., Canadian, and European support and yet receives de facto immunity against condemnation. BDS simply holds Israel to the same standard we are told repeatedly that we should apply to all other countries, especially

those in the Third World, and to the same standards by
which Israel defines itself as a godly land and a light unto
the nations.

The only people singling out Israel in this debate are the
ones opposed to BDS.

So, to answer the question, why Israel?: Because Israel
violates seventy-seven UN resolutions, more than any nation-
state in history; Israel has killed more than 1,500 Palestinian
children in the past fifteen years; Israel holds more than five
thousand political prisoners; Israel continues to build illegal
settlements; Israel has demolished twenty-seven thousand
homes since 1967; Israel has expropriated 250,000 acres of
land in the Occupied Territories and 390 squares miles of
land from its own Arab citizens; Israel's Prawer Plan aims
to displace tens of thousands of Palestinian Bedouins; and
Israel boasts prominent politicians who speak approvingly
of ethnic cleansing.[16] No amount of oppression in other
parts of the world absolves Israel of these misdeeds.

It is worth mentioning that the U.S. government bank-
rolls these oppressive acts of colonization.

Myth: BDS secretly aims to destroy Israel.

Reality: This argument diverts attention from substantive
discussion and toward disingenuous questions that victimize
the oppressor. BDS takes no formal position on either a
one-state/two-state solution or on the formal peace process.
It simply demands that Israel comply with the international
laws to which it is party, including the return of Palestinian
refugees, equal rights for Palestinian Israelis, and withdrawal
from Palestinian territories occupied through war.

Commenters such as Beinart claim that these demands
implicitly mean the destruction of Israel as a so-called
Jewish democracy. First of all, no actual democracy is
supposed to concern itself with demographic ratios, which
are the domain of ethnocratic states. And second, Israel's
unwillingness to practice equality is not a problem of BDS.
It is a problem of Israeli democracy.

Myth: States should not be boycotted.

Reality: Although critics of BDS accuse the movement of moral inconsistency, the argument that states should not be boycotted is myopic. Humans frequently boycott states and governments. It is useful to shift emphasis from the imperatives of individual actors onto the troublesome behavior that renders so many states boycottable. This shift removes the moral burden of state violence from the political consumer and instead applies it to systemic factors.

Myth: Academic boycott harms Israeli students and academics.

Reality: Israeli policies of discrimination harm Palestinian students and academics. It is one of the great features of BDS that it goes out of its way to protect the rights of individual Israelis. We have to remember that Israelis inhabit a position of great strength. It is a particular habit of colonial discourse to automatically empathize with the well-being of the oppressor, the one with power, rather than directing empathy to the colonized and to the powerless more generally. In any case, the only Israelis affected by BDS are those working on behalf of the Israeli government—that is, those profiting from the misery of Palestinians.

Myth: BDS is a strategy without a distinct purpose.

Reality: BDS has one ultimate purpose: to help liberate Palestinians from military occupation. The logic of the accusation that BDS has no distinct purpose arises from an unimaginative view of human relationships. Not all actions need a purpose in the linear sense of the term. And not all purposes are the result of righteous action.

We work to create community, to explore different ways of acting responsibly, to upend the tedious commonplaces of media discourse, to find alternatives to the ubiquity of corporate and military power. We do not have to go from point A to point B in a linear track. We merely have to decide that we will no longer be stuck on point A.

Ultimately, the onus is not on BDS to justify its purpose to the colonizer: stop colonizing Palestine and BDS will end.

Despite these myths circulating around BDS, the fact is that BDS works. I grant that defining whether or not an activist movement works is an ambiguous proposition, but I proffer my judgment primarily on one criterion: the amount of resources that the Israeli government and Zionist organizations around the world have devoted to delegitimizing BDS though intimidation and persuasion.

Not only have arguments against BDS been countered with precise ethical and intellectual rigor by a multitude of scholars, but a crucial point should be restated: BDS represents not the misguided inclinations of radical scholars but the will of the Palestinian people. We listen to the colonized. We hear the colonized. We heed the colonized. This is the first necessity of decolonization.

My maternal grandmother lost her home in Ein Karem, outside of Jerusalem, in 1948. She has never been compensated. Her loss has never been acknowledged by Israel. She refuses to visit an artsy, upper-class, Jewish suburb of Jerusalem that was once a Palestinian village—her ancestral home. She has neither forgotten nor forgiven. I have not forgotten, either. I am perfectly willing to forgive, but only in the presence of justice. Oppressors are not allowed to request forgiveness if they refuse to relinquish their ill-gotten power. And as history has shown, oppressors do not relinquish that power voluntarily.

I practice BDS because it is the only power I have in the face of the tremendous military and economic might of Israel and its American sponsor. It is a largely symbolic power, a nonviolent act of simple defiance, void of guns and platforms and legislation, but with enough support it has the potential to topple a colonial empire, one that yearns for the acceptance and affirmation of the same people it dismisses and displaces, and one ignorant of the fact that acceptance and forgiveness arise not from force but from a respect that must be earned through introspection and compassion.

The American Studies Association Gets a Tan

BDS encompasses racial politics beyond what first appears to be its natural purview. Yet racial politics is critical to BDS's moral and strategic identity, proving once again that the very notion of a natural purview is faulty. It is no accident that academic boycott has succeeded in associations representing fields that entail heavy emphasis on ethnic studies (BDS has strong ties to minority communities).[17] Boycott of Israeli universities can be conceptualized as an expression of the commitment to material politics in the marginalized spaces of academe.

This reality quickly became clear in the internal opposition to the ASA resolution, which exhibited a majoritarian angst surprising in its frankness. At the American Studies Association annual meeting in Washington, D.C., in November 2013, members gathered to formally debate and vote on adoption of BDS (albeit a limited version). Numerous commenters interpreted the resolution as symbolic of troublesome demographic shifts in the ASA—and in the humanities and social sciences more generally—that have led to decreased standards and radicalized curricula. Whereas the AAAS and NAISA adoptions of academic boycott can be dismissed as the rumblings of fields that are inherently politicized, and thus unimportant, American studies is supposed to be a venerable discipline with respectable origins. The resolution confirmed a deep-seated suspicion among traditionalists that the association and the field it represents have succumbed to a long-standing radical creep. Some of the response to the resolution reflected a broader anxiety about demographic shifts in the U.S. population. Although disheartening, it was appropriate that the response occurred within a group devoted to the field of American studies.

Noting that the American Studies Association's consideration of BDS had rendered the organization "utterly foolish," scholar Stephen Whitfield wrote, "What seems to be the case is the emergence of Ethnic Studies may have tilted the organization heavily in favor of people of color, in this case the Palestinians."[18] Another American studies scholar, Richard Slotkin, offered a comparable observation:

> the boycott is morally obtuse. Asked why Israel is singled out, when so many other states are worse violators of human rights and UN resolutions, ASA President Curtis Marez answered "one has to start somewhere." So Israel—not Bashar Assad's Syria, or Khamenei's Iran; not the People's Republic of China

which commits cultural genocide in Tibet; or Cuba, which remains a police state and persecutes dissidents and homosexuals; not even North Korea, most people's notion of hell on earth. The choice seems either arbitrary, or a reflection of ideological bias.[19]

Slotkin reinforces a binary between a type of premodern savagery, as evidenced by his conventional examples of Third World oppression, and the more normative violence of democratic overzealousness. As to his argument, it is worth pointing out that American universities have no partnerships with institutions in Syria, Cuba, Iran, and North Korea, the four countries on his list that are already subject to American sanctions and boycott.

Both arguments produce a dichotomy between acceptable and unacceptable forms of state violence. Whitfield's displeasure with the resolution leads to an overt dismissal of Palestinians and other people of color, centering a view of normative whiteness. Slotkin evokes the traditional logic and language of right-wing attacks on the modern university as a politicized space of leftist propaganda, a discourse that nearly always entails anxiety about minority narratives. This evocation is clear in his phrase "ideological bias," a truism that has been thoroughly decimated as tendentious in American studies. Ideological bias presupposes a detached knowledge that can be ascertained by disinterested observation, itself entirely missing from Slotkin's critique.

It is worthy of more than a footnote to point out that Slotkin's criticism of Curtis Marez is based on a quote insidiously taken out of context by the *New York Times* and gleefully repeated by numerous writers as evidence of the ASA's inherent biases, including anti-Semitism.[20] The full passage from the *Times,* later added to the story, where it was originally omitted, reads: "[Marez] argued that the United States has 'a particular responsibility to answer the call for boycott because it is the largest supplier of military aid to the state of Israel.' While acknowledging that the same could be said of a number of oppressive governments, past and present, he said that in those countries, civil society groups had not asked his association for a boycott, as Palestinian groups have."[21]

The ASA resolution, then, not only represented an articulation of disciplinary ethics, but reproduced in microcosm the conditions of white flight that have so prominently defined the American landscape. BDS is not merely a tactic to pressure Israel; it also symbolizes radical forms of engagement anathema to those who believe, even if implicitly, that it is distasteful to disrupt the status quo. As Richard Behar declaimed in *Forbes*:

> By all appearances, the expressions of outrage have left ASA's incoming president, NYU professor Lisa Duggan—plus the other 17 über-radical colleagues on the "national council" who voted unanimously for the boycott—unmoved. They don't care that they have torpedoed ASA's reputation (what was left of it). It seems she and her national council took it as a badge of honor, proof of their righteousness. (If "establishment" is upset, and not a single council-comrade voted against the resolution, they must be right! Right?)[22]

The resolution helped arrange the tea leaves. Those who did not like what those tea leaves portended were overwhelmingly white and repeatedly invoked the tropes of a purer, more respectable academe in order to persuade. These days such tropes rely in no small part on positioning oneself on the right side of modernity.

I attended and spoke at an open forum the ASA National Council hosted the evening before it was to meet to discuss the proposed boycott resolution in Washington. In order to accommodate as many voices as possible, the council randomly selected speakers who had placed their names in a box as they entered the room. The ballroom in which the open forum occurred was packed, with people sitting on the stairs and standing in the back. (Its listed capacity is 750.) I watched in mild shock as speaker after speaker expressed support for the resolution and for a vision of American studies that puts the field in conversation with broader decolonization efforts. Accounts of the numbers differ slightly, but at least thirty-seven people spoke in favor of the resolution, while at most seven spoke against it. Those who spoke in favor received widespread applause, while those opposed were met with the spectacle of lonely, scattered clapping echoing sadly throughout the sizable room. In that moment, American studies ceased to be American; it was busy performing quintessentially inter/national work. The demography of the gathering was trenchant, as dozens of young scholars of various ethnic backgrounds took the microphone and urged the council to adopt the resolution.

Demography is important beyond its metonymic relationship with majoritarian angst. BDS has illuminated a number of interesting phenomena often overlooked in assessment of the cultural politics of the Israel–Palestine conflict. Take, for instance, the significant opposition to BDS among American Jews (though support for BDS is also significant in the same community). It can be read in many ways: as emotional attachment to Israel; as socialized affinity; as anti-Arab racism; as existential fear of Israel's destruction; as the notion of Israel as a symbol of cultural identity; as capitulation to familial pressure; as moral and philosophical devotion to Zionism. Depending on the context, any of these factors might explain one's displeasure with BDS (or some combination of these factors in tandem). The uneven relationship between American Jews and white normativity plays a considerable role, if only tacitly. Through the corresponding factors of Zionist devotion and the mainstreaming of Zionism as an expression of American values, Jews have positioned themselves as normatively white, though the specters of anti-Semitism and marginalization never quite abate. Much opposition to BDS tacitly aspires to reinforce the spaces of white normativity, in which Jews occupy, at best, a tenuous position. Israel has helped to make Jews white in America; criticism of Israel in turn threatens to undermine that precarious status. The racial politics of academic boycott is often subsumed by more explicit concerns such as academic freedom and international law, but ultimately that politics is a defining feature of the discursive arenas in which boycott exists.

We therefore find ourselves confronted by an inter/national dialectic. In Slotkin's statement against the resolution, he suggests that "boycott is a case of 'going abroad in search of monsters to destroy.'" Does the resolution really go abroad? In what ways do static and statist notions of geopolitical space impede our understanding of BDS as a set of extraterritorial practices? Can, or should, it orient us in the landscapes of American colonization? In the following section, I argue that even when its advocates do not recognize that BDS speaks directly to Indigeneity in America, that is precisely what it does—often implicitly, but in ways we must work to make explicit.

Boycott the United States?

A common argument against BDS is that targeting Israel is hypocritical given the United States' colonial practices and aggressive foreign policy, not to mention its profound influence on global affairs, including massive economic, military, and rhetorical support for Israel. The argument is weak because it actively evades discussion of Israel's actions and legal practices, but it is nevertheless worth considering, though in a slightly different incarnation. Rather than evoke the United States as a counterpoint to Israel, we can examine it as a progenitor of Israeli oppression and thus a necessary site of analytic and political engagement.

We need to recall that BDS is not a blanket tactic. It devotes energy to what its practitioners consider legitimate targets: institutions complicit in state violence and/or military occupation, and in spaces where pressure might effectively induce material change. BDS does not extend to everything Israeli. It leaves the vast majority of Israeli society unmolested. It addresses state violence and the institutions that sustain it, but only insofar as its philosophy and resources allow it to act—it is not as extensive in practice as it is in principle. In short, there is no boycott of Israel; there are a series of interrelated boycotts against certain institutions associated with the Israeli government (and against the government itself).

This distinction is crucial to analysis of the viability of boycotting the United States. BDS does not target all elements of Israel, so it is not terribly different—in the limited sense of performing an action within a national geography—from the dozens of boycotts of American companies and institutions in effect at any given moment. If we eliminate consumer and entertainment boycotts from consideration, there is still plenty of evidence that the United

States hosts rich sites of political action comparable to the work of BDS. Recent boycotts have implicated weapons manufacturers, companies practicing labor exploitation, fossil fuels, and fast food restaurants. Boycott, then, is a significant feature of American political life.

The factor that separates Israel is that the state has been subject to *academic* boycott, a seemingly unprecedented move (although in reality boycotts of universities have plenty of precedent). Yet the United States has hosted various types of what can rightly be called academic boycott, even if those movements did not employ the titular nomenclature. Arizona, for instance, has been boycotted in two instances, one during the period in which the state refused to recognize Martin Luther King Jr. Day and the other when it passed SB 1070, the controversial law that demanded racial profiling, in 2011. The boycotts included colleges; numerous scholarly associations refused to hold conventions in the state. Various groups organized boycotts of Columbia University in 2007 in response to its hosting of a speech by Iran president Mahmoud Ahmadinejad. In 2014, workers at a university-owned DoubleTree Hotel led a boycott of Harvard because of poor working conditions. Also in 2014 (and continuing as of this writing), professors from across various disciplines enacted a boycott against the University of Illinois at Urbana-Champaign because of its administrative abrogation of academic freedom and faculty governance. Although it would be inaccurate to ascribe uniformity to these boycotts, their levels of similarity are of less interest than the mere fact of their existence.

Furthermore, if we think of boycotts as a type of pressure intended to generate a particular material result, or even as a discourse that intervenes in debate, then it would not be preposterous to point out that Zionists have long practiced de facto boycotts. These boycotts have not arisen from civil society or grassroots communities—hence my calling them "de facto"—but they have certainly been effective in marginalizing pro-Palestine narratives and Palestinians themselves. They are often centrally organized and well funded, including groups like StandWithUs, the David Project, the Anti-Defamation League, the Simon Wiesenthal Center, and AMCHA. Beyond their obvious political disagreement with BDS, the two movements differ structurally: while BDS has a clear set of principles and an aversion to discipline enforced by state institutions, movements to punish Palestinian students and faculty take their cue from on high. Their actions are often dishonest and punitive. They deploy micro-aggression as a form of normative civility and summon institutional authority to execute political aspirations.

Zionist pressure has long affected hiring decisions, curricula, awards selections, notions of civility and collegiality, access to resources, and tenure and promotion reviews within academia. Much of this activity happens behind the scenes, or through repetition of commonsensical values, and is thus unnoticed, but the collective experience of Palestine advocates on campus bespeaks an embargo on ideas and actual bodies more repressive than even the false outcomes predicted by opponents of academic boycott. I do not suggest that this repressive activity constitutes a coherent boycott, but these semantic nuances do little to assuage the suffering of Palestinians (and Arabs and Muslims more broadly) in American universities. Zionism entails structural and material aspirations in educational systems. It is joined by hundreds of other forces doing the same.

Ultimately, I urge us to discard the ahistorical notion that campuses are neutral spaces of objective merit. Individuals rise and fall based on complex intersections of discourse and economy. Implicit and explicit pressures of intellectual conformity have affected the university since its inception. If anything, academic boycott is a corrective to unnamed modes of discursive policing by making its appeals public and offering rationales for a sort of material engagement anathema to the default norms of objectivity. The objective already engages material realities, but it conceptualizes the relationship as detached. BDS proponents are therefore more attuned to and responsible for the indispensability of academic freedom than those who cloak anxiety about deviant ideas in the high-minded language of tolerance and inclusivity, the terminologies of administrative entrenchment.

The specificity of BDS to Palestine renders it limited as a site of universal analysis. The boycotts we have seen on college campuses exist, or existed, around a cross section of tactics and issues.

There is no shortage of injustice domestically or internationally to condemn. (One of the arguments against BDS is that it "singles out" Israel.) The call to undertake BDS came from Palestine. The call does not represent the totality of Palestinian society, but it has enough grassroots support in Gaza, the West Bank, Israel, and the refugee camps to generate legitimacy. When Palestinian Authority President Mahmoud Abbas criticized BDS in 2014, he was shortly thereafter rebuffed by his own parties, Fatah and the Palestine Liberation Organization (PLO).[23] Although BDS has not earned consensus among Palestinian intellectuals and activists, it is now a major element of political life in Palestine. This context informs the performance of academic boycott in the United States. It is not a context for all boycotts in the United States.

The call from Palestine is of particular import. The academic boycott of Israel does not preclude action vis-à-vis other oppressive geographies. The same relationships of civil society and scholarly engagement would prevail. The 2011 boycott of Arizona, for instance, never developed into a wide-ranging or permanent action because civil society institutions in the state came to organize around different imperatives. A major reason that the Native American and Indigenous Studies Association (NAISA) held its annual gathering in Tucson shortly after SB 1070 despite a burgeoning boycott is that local leaders and institutions, including Native communities, requested that the conference proceed. On the other hand, the boycott of the University of Illinois at Urbana-Champaign (UIUC) arises from conversation with faculty on campus displeased with their administration's behavior. Although as of this writing the parameters of the boycott are ill-defined, and the campus is divided about its appropriateness or desirability, people at other campuses largely follow the counsel of their colleagues at UIUC.

These examples contain much more shading than my brief synopsis allows, but as broad propositions they affirm the point that academic boycotts are rarely unidirectional. They emerge from dialogue among the affected parties inside institutions and concerned observers beyond those institutions. A mutual reliance thus emerges: the affected group influences extraneous sites of action while outside groups influence the tone and tenor of solidarity work. The adjective "solidarity" (as when used as a noun) may not be enough to fully delineate the dynamic. "Ally" is a less viable term. Something of a comradeship exists in these relations. Even comradeship is unsatisfying, however, though it points to a mutuality whose insinuations are morally and philosophically attractive.

Kinship might be a useful word to describe the interplay of subject and actor in decolonial communities, as well as (perceived or real) affinities among colonized groups themselves. It cannot be (or is not now) a universal material reality, but we can conceptualize it as an aspiration. Kinship bespeaks investment not in identical narratives, but in organizing for a future that envisions a life distinct from the common sense of neoliberal and colonial political systems. A sense of kinship with colleagues in Palestine guides many academic boycott advocates. That sense of kinship often finds expression in communities challenging systematic state violence in America. Kinship is more than an emotion, though. It entails the intellectual rigors of theorization and political labor. It also entails the immanence of disagreement and the primacy of difference as a prerequisite to inter/national familiarity. Academic boycott enacts these processes.

Locating difference is an effective means of discovering commonality. Difference, in any case, does not preclude solidarity, but can, if treated intelligently, enhance it. The vibrant nature of both cultural practice and activist work renders notions of "likeness" and "difference" unstable, subject to the shifts of temporal dynamism. We must reinvigorate our connections. We must constantly discover the unexamined. We must assess our mutual relationships to colonial power rather than lionizing our boundless minutiae. BDS has been an effective, though not ideal, site for staging those relationships.

BDS informs processes of American decolonization. It needs to anatomize its own efforts, particularly in its desire to avoid operating through the conceits of liberal multiculturalism, and pursue its goals through a devoted Indigenous groundwork. The participation of Indigenous peoples is central to this project. BDS can thus be viewed, and practiced, as an articulation of Native nationalism. That is to say, the Native can participate in BDS not merely to resist Israeli colonization, but to affirm American decolonization.

Boycotting Statehood in Service of Native Nationhood

The word *nationalism* will never be without controversy. Many people of the Left, including scholars, dislike it in ways that can appear visceral because of its association with colonization, patriotism, and discrimination. That those meanings attend the word makes it difficult to refigure as an analytic frame. The word has a long history in Native studies that allows us to recover a tradition rather than reconfigure vocabulary. It is in the context of nation building and its challenges that BDS and Native nationalism intersect.

We can speak of Native nationalism in two senses: first, as the practice of nationalist politics—that is, the politics of aspirations to nationhood—and, second, as a form of support for nationalist politics. These two aspects inform the conditions of inter/nationalism, by which an account of strategic possibility can be performed. Recent scholarship in Indigenous studies explores these conditions and possibilities. As Alyosha Goldstein points out, "Bridging the study of North American settler colonialism and U.S. overseas occupation provides a means with which to address both the incongruities and fault lines of the U.S. nation-state and the determined construction of national singularity, coherence, and continuity"[24] Goldstein evokes the usefulness of disruption, intellectual and geopolitical, as a way to complicate tidy narratives of colonial belonging. From these disruptions emerge a destabilization of settler identity and attendant opportunities to undermine the mythologies of singular pasts and predestined futures.

Jennifer Nez Denetdale affirms Goldstein's argument: "Raising questions about how the imposition of Western democratic ideals about nation and sovereignty on tribal nations have transformed our relationships to each other is an act of decolonization, for then we have space to reflect on the present state of our respective nations and a future where our citizens live according to our traditional principles."[25] Denetdale raises this point in the context of Diné (Navajo) self-government, but her interpretation of decolonization as a relational project offers a strong framework for inter/national communication. The first necessity, she observes, is extricating the Indigenous society from the colonial apparatus it inherited and incorporates into its governing practices: "[T]he formations of tribal nations are founded on Western democratic frameworks and therefore have inherited structures that reproduce patriarchy to perpetuate gender inequality, sexism, and homophobia.[26]

This inheritance is crucial to our understanding of decolonization. We can add to Denetdale's list neocolonialism, racism, and free-market capitalism. Because of these factors, scholars must conceptualize ways to pursue national aspirations that do not merely reproduce colonial structures. Inter/national approaches offer one such opportunity. They supplement a large body of work in American Indian studies exploring the disjunctions between tradition and political imagination.

Jodi Byrd has assessed these matters. In *The Transit of Empire* she writes, "To be in transit is to be active presence in a world of relational movements and countermovements. To be in transit is to exist relationally, multiply."[27] She notes: "As the administrative colonialism of European empires dismantled after World War II, the deep settler and arrivant colonialisms continued unabated within the post- and neocolonial geographies of the global South that are now reconfigured to bear the brunt of the economic, environmental, and militaristic needs of the global North."[28]

Byrd's passages are of a mind with Kevin Bruyneel's analysis of colonial boundaries:

> The imposition of colonial rule denotes the effort of the Unites States to narrowly bound indigenous political status in space and time, seeking to limit the ability of indigenous people to define their own identity and develop economically and politically on their own terms. In resistance to this colonial rule, indigenous political actors work across American spatial and temporal boundaries, demanding rights and resources from the liberal democratic settler-state while also challenging the imposition of colonial rule in their lives.[29]

Byrd and Bruyneel approach questions of sovereignty and liberation from different points of view, but both desire stronger emphasis on contextual issues of global import that are dynamic and incongruous. Their visions of a meaningful Native self-determination involve more than mere affirmation of treaty rights, an approach Glen Coulthard likewise urges in *Red Skin, White Masks*.[30] They also involve dismantling the systems of economic, racial, sexual, and legal iniquity that persist through ongoing colonization and its internalization by those seeking alternatives to the colonial project.

The U.S. state is a global phenomenon. It maintains its economy through corporate appropriation of resources, particularly in the Southern Hemisphere. Its military occupies five continents. Its intelligence services meddle in the affairs of poorer, weaker states. It installs (or maintains) repressive leadership in other countries based on the preferences of the U.S. business elite. It relies on torture as a form of discipline (not only against the tortured, but against those who fear torture as a response to anti-U.S. activity). There are few areas of the world in which the United States is not at least indirectly involved. It monitors the globe and makes any necessary corrections to aberrance from its preferred neoliberal economy.

It is anathema to conceptualize American decolonization as merely a continental project. American colonization is an international phenomenon, attuned to the necessities of eliminating inter/national praxis. The United States itself, like all nation-states arising from the violence of modernity, is but a composite of colonial interplay. As Iris Marion Young explains,

> One story of World History describes a lineal progression where universal values of liberty, democracy, technology, and economic development born in Western Europe spread around the world through the power and knowledge of European nations. In this story the colonized peoples of the world usually appear as objects of action, those upon whom the power and influence of the West is exercised, usually for good, sometimes for ill. While the story includes the encounter and conflict of cultures, it does not depict the ideas, practices, institutions, and events of the Europeans as objects of and influenced by the subjectivity of the non-European Others.[31]

U.S. colonization likewise extends to the Caribbean and the Pacific. We can therefore view the United States as a destabilized site of settler identity in two senses: first, in terms of the land it has conquered, and, second, in light of its reliance on a particular global order to rejuvenate itself. America is an invention of the U.S. settler; it is also the burden of the world. Native nationalism opposes a colonization whose influence traverses the settler's physical location.

The usefulness of BDS to this process depends on its ability to develop the same critique raised by Byrd, Bruyneel, and Coulthard. As Omar Barghouti, a leader of the moment, stresses,

> in contexts of colonial oppression, intellectuals, especially those who advocate and work for justice, cannot be just — or mere — intellectuals in the abstract sense; they cannot but be immersed in some form or another of activism, to learn from fellow activists through real-life experiences, to widen the horizon of their sources of inspiration, and to organically engage in effective, collective emancipatory processes aimed at reaching justice without self-indulgence, complacency, or ivory-towerness that might otherwise blur their moral vision.[32]

Barghouti's desire is ambitious, but instructive. In order to enact it, BDS cannot be limited to the physical sphere of Israel's location but must encounter Israel as it actually exists in the world. Its location is not nebulous: it exists in spaces of militarized repression, counterrevolution, and garrison settlement. The Atlantic only symbolically divides the United States and Israel. BDS is concerned with articulations of U.S. and Canadian colonization whether or not its practitioners are aware of that concern. It is, in any case, a good idea to continue making explicit these connections and to better center them in the consciousness of the movement. Native nationalism remains the prerogative of the Indigenous subject; BDS supplements and articulates Native nationalism only by Indigenous participation in its visions for inter/national decolonization.

"Ivory-towerness" is a great term to describe an oblique academic sensibility, one desirous of disinterest, civility, and moderation, the main elements of colonial decorum. I cannot quite define it (and Barghouti does not offer a specific definition), and yet its meaning is clear: it denotes an illusion of responsibility, a self-righteous perpetuation of authority, an endless rehearsal of tedious nostalgia. Barghouti implies a distinction between the interests of the university and the imperatives of the activist. Eroding that distinction in both thought and practice is a worthwhile enterprise.

BDS Deterritorialized

How might BDS productively challenge these phenomena? First, we can recognize that recent scholarship in American Indian studies tethers articulations of Native nationalism to inter/nationalist dynamics. The scholarship thus foregrounds BDS. It prefigures the conditions that give rise to Zionist settlement. Native nationalism threatens the ascendancy of the Israeli state as surely as it does the authority of the United States.

I am not demanding that Natives take up BDS. Rather, I suggest that BDS inherently encounters Indian country and the imaginaries of America; its advocates in the United States should therefore engage American Indian studies scholarship and further explore the possibilities of contributing to the decolonial process in America. Such a move is not an abdication of responsibility to Palestine but an avowal of the responsibility to liberate the ground on which we stand—likewise an effective means to achieve Palestinian liberation. Those elements of Native nationalism and BDS that have long been implicit can be made explicit. The process is complicated, and might at times become messy, but it would mark an important development in the ability of BDS to conjoin itself to a global politics of Indigenism rather than to a liberal notion of multicultural dialogue. Many Indigenous scholars—Robert Warrior, J. Kēhaulani Kauanui, Vince Diaz, JoAnne Barker, Aileen Moreton-Robinson, Lisa Kahaleole Hall—practice BDS in part because of this recognition.

Mike Krebs and Dana Olwan note, in the context of Canadian settler colonization, that

> Palestinian organising in Canada has a long way to go by way of supporting indigenous struggles and forming real alliances that do not mimic or reproduce settler colonial relationships between colonisers and the colonised. There is still some resistance to making explicit connections between these struggles within Palestine solidarity circles in Canada. It is also our view

that Canadian Palestinians have not yet confronted their own
relationship to settlement in Canada and have not yet clarified
how they position themselves in relation to the European settler
project here.[33]

The critique holds for the United States, too. I have heard too many
Palestinians invoke U.S. settlement as a thing of the past in order to
appeal to the urgency of ending Israeli occupation. But this urgency
should not allow us to omit ongoing colonization in the United
States and Canada. Krebs and Olwan warn against the tokeniza-
tion of indigenes by inviting one or a few to speak at Palestine
solidarity events.[34] Palestine solidarity activists must challenge the
authority of state institutions that participate in, and legitimize,
U.S. and Canadian colonialism rather than buttressing those institutions by invoking them as sites of redress. BDS is uniquely positioned to shift the discourse because of its tremendous ability to
attract supporters and shepherd issues of colonization and decolonization into spaces in which they are normally unwelcome.

Here is a simple way to think about this imperative: we expect
visitors to Palestine, or expats in Palestine, to accommodate Palestinian narratives and aspirations without dictating to them the
terms of their liberation or ignoring their experiences of oppression for the sake of the outsider's convenience. We thus have no
right to expect anything less of ourselves in America.

Krebs and Olwan argue that gendered violence has been a crucial feature of the settler state. As a result, "settler colonialism does
not operate independently of the histories and legacies of genocide,
gendered and sexual violence, cultural appropriation, and land con-
fiscation."[35] They urge emphasis on the special role this gendered
and sexual violence has played in formations of colonial logic and
practice (something I take up more fully in chapter 5). Krebs and
Olwan do not disavow the centrality of racism and capitalism to
the settlement of North America and Palestine; they point out that
sexual violence frames both phenomena and has not received the
full attention it deserves. That sexual violence remains a serious
problem in North America illuminates the survival of colonialist
attitudes. Sexual violence occurs everywhere, but the conceits of

modernity conceptualize it as an aberration rather than a constituent feature of the modern. Here is the greatest value of Krebs and Olwan's argument: they refuse to isolate the state from the effects of colonization. Pursuing justice, in this schema, is not to reform the United States or Canada but to decolonize it. This argument tracks with Mishuana Goeman's important work on women and Native decolonization, in which she examines "Native conceptualizations of space . . . [that] (re)map a history of what Mary Louise Pratt terms a 'European planetary consciousness,' a consciousness that is deeply patriarchical."[36]

It follows, then, that to properly address problems of sexism, sexual violence, classism, racism, and so forth, we must interrogate the problem of ongoing U.S. and Canadian colonization. The distinctions among modes of colonization help sharpen our focus. Waziyatawin suggests that "[i]f the US was still in its heyday of its expansionist frenzy but had twenty-first century technology, I imagine the visible effects of colonization across the continent would look very similar to those in Palestine."[37] Other distinctions include the ability of the United States and Canada to attract huge numbers of immigrants, whereas Israel has difficulty generating mass immigration; population differences in balance of origin and geography (Arabs vastly outnumber Israelis); the geopolitical dynamics that prevail today as opposed to prior centuries; and the remarkably varied and expansive American landscape in contrast to the small size of the Holy Land (despite its impressive climatological and topographical variance).

For these reasons, comparative analyses of America and Palestine largely operate at the level of imagination, by which I do not mean the invention of images but the superimposition of discrete historical epochs onto a specific context of settler colonization. Despite the vast differences of U.S./Canadian and Israeli colonialism, we can imagine sameness based on the survival of certain narratives across the centuries. In order to fully realize the dispossession of Palestinians, BDS must contextualize a particular transatlantic bond, what Hilton Obenzinger calls a "Holy Land mania" in *American Palestine,* whose origin predates the advent of the nation-state in America and Palestine. (It also must be attentive to Transpacific bonds.) Native nationalism is not simply an opportunity for theoretical framing but a necessary condition of Palestine's liberation. The colonial underpinnings of democratic logic in the American and Canadian political systems, deployed as the normative solution to conflict, bring this reality into sharp relief.

Waziyatawin identifies a crucial feature of the colonial imagination: "Of course the Zionist ideology that underpins Israeli colonial occupation is the same as the Manifest Destiny ideology that underpinned US colonial expansion, in that both are based on a belief in a divinely-sanctioned right to occupy someone else's land. The legal systems arising from these colonial contexts are specifically designed to codify colonial claims. Like in Palestine, every Indigenous nation in what is now the US faced similar actions of legalised land theft."[38] She notes that all Israeli "colonial efforts are designed to assert a claim to land, while simultaneously attempting to make the indigenous the foreigner. Similar tactics characterise colonial claiming and renaming of Indigenous spaces in the US. Accompanying the theft of our lands and the implementation of major campaigns of ethnic cleansing was always a process of ideological colonisation."[39]

These observations allow us to envision the practice of BDS on American landscapes as a dual responsibility: beyond its obvious focus on Palestinian liberation, it can produce useful inquiry into the relationships of diasporic Palestinians (and their allies) with the settler communities they inhabit. The movement can articulate Native nationalism by deterritorializing its strategies from a physical geography and working to render that geography unexceptional. An unexceptional geography concedes that settler colonization is not limited to a singular domain and in turn undermines the mythological narratives of settlement. Krebs and Olwan's appeal to highlight issues of sexual violence and racism that comprise the anatomy of garrison settlement informs this goal.

Lest I be misread: BDS activists and scholars, in Palestine and America, have undertaken these analytic moves, in many cases with inspiring sophistication. My concern is a sustained engagement with greater emphasis on global Indigenous spaces as against the appropriation of BDS into the pieties of rapprochement and institutional civility. To borrow from Joseph Massad:

As I have written and explained since the signing of the 1993 Oslo accords, all the "solutions" offered by Western and Arab governments and Israeli and PA [Palestinian Authority] liberals to end the so-called "Palestinian–Israeli conflict" are premised on guaranteeing Israel's survival as a racist Jewish state unscathed. All "solutions" that do not offer such a guarantee are dismissed *a priori* as impractical, unpragmatic and even anti-Semitic. The recent attempts to co-opt BDS for that very same goal are in line with this commitment.[40]

Massad speaks of the versions of BDS that limit it to a boycott of products from the occupied West Bank or those evoked by state actors in symbolic votes for Palestinian statehood (something a number of European Union countries did in 2014). Massad desires more emphasis on decolonization through the centering of Palestinian belonging and the right of return (a legal and moral concept that would enable refugees to return to their original homes in Palestine).

Yet any reliance on state protocol is a tricky proposition, something to which Massad has repeatedly pointed in his work. The inadequacy of state protocol is usually the impetus for a boycott in the first place. Judith Butler highlights this reality, claiming that Palestinian intellectuals and activists

> have come to the understanding that nation-states and international bodies refuse to enforce those international laws and norms that would bring the state of Israel into compliance. BDS is the option that non-state actors have, that populations have who are operating in universities, social movements, legal organizations, citizens, partial citizens and the undocumented. The BDS movement has become the most important contemporary alliance calling for an end to forms of citizenship based on racial stratification, insisting on rights of political self-determination for those for whom such basic freedoms are denied or indefinitely suspended, insisting as well on substantial ways of redressing the rights of those forcibly and/or illegally dispossessed of property and land (even as there are open debates at the present about what form that should take).[41]

Butler evokes the inter/national nature of BDS by pointing to amorphous subjects beyond Palestine. Indeed, by not naming specific geographies, she draws attention to broader matters of dispossession and stratification framing Israel's occupation. Palestine becomes integrated into worldly systems of political and economic oppression.

Such integration is evident in the 2014 NAISA pledge to adhere to the academic boycott of Israel. The NAISA Council's statement proclaims, "As the elected council of an international community of Indigenous and allied non-Indigenous scholars, students, and public intellectuals who have studied and resisted the colonization and domination of Indigenous lands via settler state structures throughout the world, we strongly protest the illegal occupation of Palestinian lands and the legal structures of the Israeli state that systematically discriminate against Palestinians and other Indigenous peoples."[42] The council renders key nouns—land, state structure, legal structure—in the plural, intimating that settler colonization affects various Indigenous groups simultaneously. This intimation represents more than an integration of Palestine into Native spaces; it highlights an activist and scholarly ethics that values structural analysis of state power and Indigenous resistance. The council notes that Israeli colonization violates not merely the integrity of Palestinians but that of Indigenous peoples throughout the world.

J. Kēhaulani Kauanui develops this theme in an article for *Social Text* titled "One Occupation." She describes a meeting with Palestinian activists in Haifa, an Israeli port city that was once overwhelmingly Arab until it suffered ethnic cleansing in 1948: "Their penetrating critiques and our productive dialogue ultimately strengthened my understanding of the situation of fragmentation on the ground in Palestine, and of the need to grapple with this complexity to address what is, after all, one occupation."[43] To conceptualize all of Palestine as occupied, rather than merely the West Bank and Gaza Strip, is not necessarily a radical notion—it is a common viewpoint in the Southern Hemisphere—but it signals the potential for radical approaches to decolonization. In America, the equivalent would be a refusal to limit Native nationalism to treaty rights, opting to treat decolonial thought and practice as a continental project instead. The notion of "one occupation" extends beyond Palestine. It is an inter/national concern.

"One occupation" can reference the archetypal strategies of settler colonization: dehumanization of natives; naturalization of conquest; legal iniquity; racism; binaristic thought; disingenuousness; legislative malfeasance; treachery; systemic violence; messianism; or falsified history. Settler colonization pervades the ethos of international ruling bodies, human rights organizations, and NGOs. True liberation has never occurred through the legislative maneuvers of civilized men in designer suits. Indigenous peoples across the world face multitudinous forms of occupation, but ultimately the practices entailed by occupation amount to one imperative and seek an identical result.

Kauanui and other Indigenous practitioners of BDS are not simply concerned with an iteration of solidarity. They view BDS as compatible with, or a supplement to, their work in Indigenous communities. The notion of BDS I put forward—as extensions of the work already done by Bill Mullen, Robin D. G. Kelley, David Lloyd, Sunaina Maira, and others—prioritizes economic, racial, sexual, and geographic issues in addition to its traditional uses of rights-based discourse. That is to say, it disaggregates BDS from the provincialism of a singular geography and asks its advocates in the United States and Canada to subvert colonization wherever their feet touch the ground.

Conclusion: No Injunction

I am aware that BDS has generated opposition within Native and Indigenous communities, although, beyond some marginal actors affiliated with pro-Israel organizations, that opposition has less to do with an inherent affinity for Israel than with a tepid outlook about the viability of BDS. Some Native Christians identify with Israel for religious reasons. Some Native and Indigenous scholars find BDS extraneous to their focus and yet another burden above and beyond the many issues facing their communities. Some Natives see the Israel–Palestine conflict as unduly acrimonious and divisive. And some see the potential of Israel/Palestine to dominate professional conversation.

Thus, I am not asking Native or Indigenous people to endorse or take up BDS. I am theorizing a better way to practice BDS that engages Natives on terms they consider palatable. And I am thinking about ways to put BDS practitioners in the United States and Canada in more stable conversation with matters of American decolonization. Our imperative is to articulate possibilities, rather than, say, demanding participation or performing an injunction. Returning to the notion of kinship, the mere potential for a sustainable filiation arises from the comfort to speak and a desire to listen. Decolonization fundamentally is about disordering the territories of colonial occupation—mentally, physically, spiritually, emotionally, imaginatively, economically, sexually, and intellectually. BDS will not remain a decolonial enterprise unless it continues to pursue the broader problems in which Israeli ethnic cleansing is implicated.

How can BDS act as an articulation of Native nationalism? One need merely read Indigenous analyses of BDS to find the answer. It became an articulation of Native nationalism the moment it left Palestinian civil society and entered into the vocabulary of global decolonization.

3.
ETHNIC CLEANSING AS
NATIONAL UPLIFT

■ ■ ■

I have a soft spot for forthrightness, quite independent of moral probity. Forthright presentation of viewpoints enables us to engage the ethical and philosophical content of a scholar, activist, or ideologue, even (especially) those we deplore. It saves us the hassle of translating the platitudes of the liberal colonizer, which usually ends with the liberal-colonizer-cum-savior outraged that anybody could possibly misread his altruistic intent.

It is therefore a terrible pleasure for me to read Andrew Jackson and Ze'ev Vladimir Jabotinsky. Both played central roles in horrible acts of ethnic cleansing, Jackson in the Trail of Tears and Jabotinsky in the 1948 *nakba* (catastrophe), when more than seven hundred thousand Palestinian Arabs were expelled from their homes. There are major differences between the two: Jabotinsky was never formally an Israeli politician, much less a head of state. He died before Israel came into existence. He was a politician, however, though he is best conceptualized as a military strategist and theorist of Zionism. Jackson is known less for his political theory than for his violent stint as U.S. president, but he left behind a significant body of writing and oration. Jackson presided over the Trail of Tears whereas Jabotinsky founded the organizations—the Irgun militia in particular—that eventually led to the establishment of Likud, Israel's foremost conservative party. Jackson often played the role of oblique or dissimulating politician, as opposed to the always-forthright Jabotinsky, but he sometimes spoke bluntly, as in the speeches I analyze in this chapter. Both men were prominent advocates of the removal of native populations. Both men are so compelling in part because they were intelligent, which is not to be confused with principled.

Their thinking around matters of ethnic cleansing intersects in fascinating ways. There is no evidence that Jabotinsky was familiar with Jackson's writing or policy, which makes these intersections all the more interesting. The two were not contemporaries, but in any case did not need to encounter each other because the ideologies they developed and maintained are of comparable purpose. They reify the logic of settler colonization and theorize the necessity of violence in the development of a sustainable modernity. This logic is not limited to the details of ethnic cleansing. Analysis of their discourse reveals important elements of the U.S.-Israeli "special relationship." Colonial ideologies cannot be said to exist outside of time, but they never exist solely within their own epoch, either. As Steven Newcomb explains,

> [T]he Judeo-Christian worldview, traced in particular to the Genesis story of the Chosen People and the Promised Land, serves as the *religious* backdrop and conceptual basis of U.S. federal Indian law and policy. It is on the basis of that biblical source of ideas that the United States claims to be "the Sovereign" with "ascendency" (a right of domination) over originally free and still rightfully free Indian nations. That Old Testament religio-political worldview is the background source of the United States' claim that the U.S. federal government has an unquestionable and unchallengeable right of "plenary power" over Indian nations and a power of "dominium" ("ultimate dominion") over the territories over Indian nations.[1]

In reading Jackson and Jabotinsky, I focus on a few phenomena. I am particularly interested in the (unacknowledged) assumptions underlying their discourses, which produce a remarkable dialectic whose simple complexity I illuminate. I am also interested in unpacking their staunch belief in both the necessity and imminence of modernity, and the centrality of violence in realizing its materialization. They cannot conceive of their colonial ambitions without the psychic evanescence of the Native. (In Jabotinsky's case, "Native" refers to the indigenes of both America and Palestine. His justification for the cleansing of Palestinians relies on a conception of Native dispossession that is simultaneously ignorant and archetypal.) Finally, Jackson and Jabotinsky are entrapped in a type of linearity that circumscribes their ability to imagine a future that precedes their appeals to genocide. Both tenuously recognize the humanity of the Native, using that recognition as the rationale for their necessary displacement. Jackson and Jabotinsky do not appeal to crude phrenological narratives, but to the realism of compassion: the Native impedes a political story that must be fulfilled. The Native must be removed, then, because of his unfortunate inability to adapt to the new reality or his unwillingness to voluntarily assent to the construction of a grander nation. Inferior biology (or even culture) is quite extraneous to this project (on the surface of their rhetoric, anyway). In this way, they helped design a strategy that would be used by numerous imperialists in the following decades.

I proceed with analysis of Jackson's "Annual Messages" regarding Indian removal, specifically the first, second, fifth, and sixth, which span the proposal of the Removal Act to its implementation (1829–34). These selections are short, as is the essay "The Iron Wall" (1923), Jabotinsky's most famous work, in which he declares the presence of Arabs incompatible with the dream of a Jewish state. Their brevity is no impediment. To the contrary, it provides a great opportunity to read closely and critically. I do not want to compare Jackson and Jabotinsky simply for the sake of illumination. Undertaking the comparison is a useful way to stake out the imperatives of decolonization by supplying the logic of ethnic cleansing with a counterweight to its apparently trenchant valuations of progress. In reality, those valuations are not at all trenchant. They presuppose our socialization into an inherently violent ethos passing itself off as benign and beneficent. Dismantling the perversity and pervasiveness of this conceit is the foundational work of decolonization.

Andrew Jackson and the Wandering Savage

At the end of 1830, on the brink of Indian removal, Andrew Jackson raised a series of rhetorical questions:

> And is it supposed that the wandering savage has a stronger attachment to his home than the settled, civilized Christian? Is it more afflicting to him to leave the graves of his fathers than it is to our brothers and children? Rightly considered, the policy of the General Government toward the red man is not only liberal, but generous. He is unwilling to submit to the laws of the States and mingle with their population. To save him from this alternative, or perhaps utter annihilation, the General Government kindly offers him a new home, and proposes to pay the whole expense of his removal and settlement.[2]

One could spend days interpreting and then countering this passage. I will try to limit analysis to my methodological scope.

The first thing of interest is Jackson's notion of a "wandering savage," which sounds much like the imagery of diasporic Jewry in both language and concept, and also the vision of Palestinians in early Zionist mythology. Jackson constructs the Natives as nomadic, unsettled, as against the stabilizing influence of the settler. He evokes an imagery that can accommodate both Jews and Palestinians in our historical consciousness because that consciousness is less reliant on cultural identity than on the temporality of nation building through capitalist practices. The savage cannot wander; he must be inert. But he cannot be settled where the new population endeavors to live. His only option is to be displaced. To do otherwise is to abdicate a natural social and economic arrangement to which all humans must submit. This arrangement only benefits the more powerful party, but the interests of power are universalized and thus made to be the basis of all projects of demographic engineering.

Jackson considers the settler's desire for the land just as strong as that of the Native. It is a valuation without an empirical basis, which is precisely its rhetorical and emotional utility. If the notion of Indigeneity relies on a land-based identity, then conceptualizing the land as an unclaimed commodity undercuts cultural and historical claims to residency. Jackson had vacated the land before the Removal Act was even passed.

To Jackson, removal is an act of altruism. (And here I cannot help but comment on the euphemistic presentation of a genocidal policy.) He endeavors to save the Indian from the brutality of history. This formulation is common among settlers. Rather than confronting their complicity, or centrality, to anything historically brutal, they treat the violence of modernity as extraneous to their own agency. Progress causes suffering; they merely seek to be progressive. Because Natives refuse to assimilate into white society, they become an existential inconvenience, a corporeal surplus, subject to the pragmatic decision making of a burgeoning imperium. The logic of capitalism informing this ethic demands that remuneration supersede empathy. When Jackson offered to pay all of the Natives' expenses, he did not include the hidden costs of ethnic cleansing in his calculation.

Of special interest in Jackson's comment are his transitory affinities. He appropriates the Indian into the image of the European immigrant; each of those immigrants is a legend who escaped Old World strife to work hard and begin life again as a New Man in a new nation he helped build from scratch. In Jackson's estimation, the U.S. government is doing the Natives a favor by compelling them to reproduce the glories of American history. It would be superfluous to spend time recounting the follies of Jackson's fantasy, but it would be too easy simply to say they make no sense. They make perfect sense in the framework of genuflection to the majesty of manifest destiny. Genocide becomes the context for civility. The Natives have no choice but to re-create the trajectory of U.S. history. It did not occur to Jackson that the trajectory of U.S. history enacted the wholesale dispossession of Indigenous peoples. (Perhaps it did occur to him, but he certainly did not expect it to occur to his audience.) Settler narratives, then, conquer the ideals of modernity, to which the Native must either submit or from which he must be banished.

This ideal permeates all iterations of settler common sense. In the same "Message," Jackson declared, "What good man would prefer a country covered with forests and ranged by a few thousand savages to our extensive Republic, studded with cities, towns, and prosperous farms embellished with all the improvements which art can devise or industry execute, occupied by more than 12,000,000 happy people, and filled with all the blessings of liberty, civilization and religion?" The crucial element of Jackson's rhetoric is his banishment of Natives from the country while pretending to embrace them and invoking the expansionist state as a site of endless opportunity. Yet Jackson tacitly forestalls either possibility. He prefaces his oratory with "what good man?" The adjective "good" suggests that anybody opposed to U.S. settlement or Indian removal is "bad," perhaps even subhuman or evil. Basic deductive reasoning allows the reader to understand Jackson's view of the Native (and, to a lesser extent, of his political opponents). Jackson reinforces the binaristic formulations that preceded his birth and that would come to predominate a century later when Jabotinsky developed his philosophy of settlement.

The presaging of Zionism is especially visible in Jackson's evocation of an industrious nation-state. It is one of the primary narratives that bind the United States and Israel in perpetual admiration. Jackson gushes about cities, farms, and industry. The United States is capitalism at work, constrained only by the savage Native and the premodenity of his condition, which he has no desire to address. In this schema, the natural, forested landscape is incomprehensible, but clearly sinful. The motivated American, this peculiar new man of destiny, is to cut, chop, and slash so the innovativeness of his character can emerge through the tactile objects of crops, neighborhoods, and factories. Jackson's utopianism, however, belies the heuristic intent of his argument. He did not lodge a jeremiad about the Native's inability to appreciate American ingenuity. He performed a version of national uplift that rallied American settlers to the reality that their national vision was incompatible with the mere presence of Indians.

His other "Annual Messages" make this clear. Here is the first one, in its entirety, delivered in 1829:

> Our conduct toward these people is deeply interesting to our national character. Their present condition, contrasted with

what they once were, makes a most powerful appeal to our sympathies. Our ancestors found them the uncontrolled possessors of these vast regions. By persuasion and force they have been made to retire from river to river and from mountain to mountain, until some of the tribes have become extinct and others have left but remnants to preserve for awhile their once terrible names. Surrounded by the whites with their arts of civilization, which by destroying the resources of the savage doom him to weakness and decay, the fate of the Mohegan, the Narragansett, and the Delaware is fast overtaking the Choctaw, the Cherokee, and the Creek. That this fate surely awaits them if they remain within the limits of the states does not admit of a doubt. Humanity and national honor demand that every effort should be made to avert so great a calamity.[3]

In the colonial imagination, ethnic cleansing is not a calamity. Allowing the Native to wither in his primordial sensibilities would be the true catastrophe. Thus violence is normalized as the progenitor of civilization. Jackson warned against the extinction of the Natives, but proposed a solution that would more efficiently make them extinct.

Jackson did not invent this approach. It was a hallmark of U.S. and Canadian colonial discourses from the moment of contact. Jackson positions those discourses in capitalist mythologies of physical and spiritual development. The violence of removal is a duty in addition to a benediction. The legal and political cultures of the United States and Canada institutionalize this mode of thought, which often acts as the default point of view vis-à-vis Native nationalism. Dale Turner contends that "the very ways that we frame the language of rights, sovereignty, and nationalism are also steeped in colonialism; yet, like the political relationship, indigenous resistance has weathered these discourses."[4] Turner encourages his readers to continue engaging the commonplaces of colonial thought, but mainly in the service of retaining connections to Indigenous traditions of thought, governance, and resistance. Jackson's "Messages" codified the norms of settlement that dictate our sense of pragmatic critique. It is a pragmatism of state violence.

To return to Jodi Byrd's notion of an empire in transit, we glean useful possibilities by considering Jackson's support of removal a transitory phenomenon. Beyond the literal transfer of populations, Jackson rationalizes a modernity based on the continual transit of settlers and their cultivation of resources. As Byrd observes, "What it means to be in transit, then, is to be in motion, to exist liminally in the ungrievable spaces of suspicion and unintelligibility. To be in transit is to be made to move."[5] The term also connotes transition, a cardinal feature of the settler's psyche. A modern citizenry relies on the perpetual transformation of the settler, which occurs only through continual motion, a primary motivation for the thirsty expropriation of land. Thus Jackson can mourn the destruction of the Native's resources while simultaneously celebrating the settler's need for resource development.

Jackson was no less determined after the Removal Act had been passed and partly implemented. His unbounded optimism had waned, however. In his "Sixth Message," in 1834, four years after passage of the act, he declared:

> I regret that the Cherokees east of the Mississippi have not yet determined as a community to remove. How long the personal causes which have heretofore retarded that ultimately inevitable measure will continue to operate I am unable to conjecture. It is certain, however, that delay will bring with it accumulated evils which will render their condition more and more unpleasant. The experience of every year adds to the conviction that emigration, and that alone, can preserve from destruction the remnant of the tribes yet living amongst us.[6]

Cherokee (and other tribal) recalcitrance had undermined Jackson's confidence. His plan was simple and logical, and yet the Natives had regrettably failed to see its wisdom. Their own stubbornness is to blame for their wretched condition. The state violence over which Jackson presided was transformed into an artful discourse of ontological innocence. The Native, on the other hand, is evil incarnate, unwilling to assume responsibility for the conditions of his suffering, even those over which he has no control. The notion of "personal responsibility" so popular today among the American

Right has a long history in the diction of American politics. It is not merely a racist concept, but one rooted in colonial values.

Again, we see the language of inevitability. Jackson was not messianic in the way of Cotton Mather, though he too had a penchant for lofty proclamations, but he held an unshakable belief in the utility of ethnic cleansing. He understood that his vision of America was unfeasible without removal. He returns to this vision repeatedly, imploring fellow politicians to intervene and do something in the absence of Indian cooperation. His urging is a rhetorical cover for his exterminationist realism. Jackson knew that Natives would not accept removal, though it is difficult to determine his level of sincerity when he extolled its ability to improve their lives. His knowledge in any case was grounded in the interests of the settler society, so his concept of improvement was inherently corrupted. Jackson's understanding that Natives would resist displacement foregrounds one of Jabotinsky's main arguments.

Although it is difficult to gauge the extent of Jackson's sincerity (or insincerity), we can make reasonable inferences based on the totality of his Messages. Here is 1833's "Fifth Message" in full:

> My original convictions upon this subject have been confirmed by the course of events for several years, and experience is every day adding to their strength. That those tribes can not exist surrounded by our settlements and in continual contact with our citizens is certain. They have neither the intelligence, the industry, the moral habits, nor the desire of improvement which are essential to any favorable change in their condition. Established in the midst of another and a superior race, and without appreciating the causes of their inferiority or seeking to control them, they must necessarily yield to the force of circumstances and ere long disappear.[7]

By this point, the Removal Act had achieved mixed success. (I deploy "success" here in the framework of the desire to cleanse large areas of Indians—in other words, how Jackson would have defined the term.) Here we find a grumpy, frustrated Jackson, much less interested in the flowery language of uplift. His discourse shifts. Rather than saying the Natives are destined for extinction because of the natural progress of modernity, he theorizes their innate inferiority as the main factor. The two explanations are not mutually exclusive. This shift is less an alteration of belief than of rhetoric. Jackson had always believed that the Indians were destined for displacement, or extinction, and frequently blamed lack of progress toward this fate on circumstance. Not long after, he began to attribute circumstance to the negative inborn characteristics of the Indian. Native inferiority is precisely the "force of circumstance" Jackson cites.

He never achieves total clarity, though. His use of *disappear* is ambivalent. Various notions of disappearance are central to colonial ideologies—disappearance, for instance, of people, ideas, identities, or ethos—and so Jackson's ambivalence could specifically reference numerous things or it could be vague on purpose. Of note is the certitude of a vanishing imperative. The Native must disappear. But what are the circumstantial factors in his disappearance? Jackson did not reveal whatever algorithm he used to balance natural causes against human agency. Nor did he reveal the temporal context for "ere long." Was he referencing the completion of the removal process? Or the dismal fate of the Natives because of the Removal Act's partial failure? We cannot know for sure. Based on a fuller spectrum of Jackson's comments, it would be reasonable to conclude that he had in mind physical extermination, whether it occurred in the Southeast or in Indian Territory (later to become the state of Oklahoma). In any case, Jackson's ambivalence reinforces rather than complicates a genocidal imperative.

Of special interest is the phrase "without appreciating the causes of their inferiority or seeking to control them." Jackson's believed firmly in Indian subhumanity, as did most of his politician colleagues. Yet he did not name the causes of that subhumanity. He intimates a failure of discipline or discretion in addition to problems of intellectual and cultural inferiority. Jackson was not particularly religious, though prevailing Christian narratives certainly influenced his thought. Nor did he resort to aggressive bombast in the manner of Theodore Roosevelt, though his zeal to practice violence against savages was no less pronounced. He did not reference phrenology or other pseudoscientific theories in his six "Messages."

It is challenging to identify a singular rationale for Jackson's racism, though it is easy to identify his racist worldview.

A good way to account for that racist worldview is to dissociate Jackson from his own personhood and instead contemplate him in the context of the political system he inhabited and represented. Jackson's racism emerged from particular conditions; it was systemic, not individual. Prevailing factors include the aggressive demands of capitalism, the primacy of an expansionist ideology, the pursuit of civility, the canonization of masculine power, and the codification of white supremacy in American national identity. Jackson's attitudes possessed a market value in the accrual of political capital. In U.S. governance, the demands of an imperium create the politician. Ethnic cleansing created Jackson.

It might not be fair to deem Jackson an exemplar of U.S. and Canadian colonization, for the process of settling the continent took many forms, not all of them in harmony. However, he articulated the necessity of ethnic cleansing as the prerequisite of a modern consciousness, one oriented around the superiority of male, Christian settlers. He also practiced that necessity with gusto. Numerous Native nations suffered tremendously as a result of the Removal Act, which easily fulfilled the criteria for genocide later developed by famed Holocaust theorist Raphael Lemkin. Natives lost enormous tracts of land to the U.S. government, which opened them to development, rendering them permanent artifacts of a new society—or, as they have been called in other contexts, facts on the ground. Native loss of life during the removal years was terrible. To Jackson, these deaths were neither immoral nor preventable. In his more reflective moments they may have been unfortunate or even tragic—not because of any problem with the philosophies of settlement, but because of the tragic misfortune of the stagnating Native.

Ze'ev Jabotinsky and the Violence of Polite Indifference

Jabotinsky was a truthful proponent of his viewpoints, yet he, like Jackson, was consummately dishonest. Born into a largely secular middle-class family in Odessa, Russian Empire (now Ukraine),

Jabotinsky joined the Zionist movement in the early twentieth century and participated as a Russian delegate to the sixth Zionist Congress in Basel, Switzerland. After settling in Palestine, Jabotinsky created a number of right-wing Zionist organizations, some of them militant. His ideas continue to influence Israeli politics and identity, though few of the state's leaders have since matched his somber intelligence. Jabotinsky's truthfulness existed primarily in one insight. As Avi Shlaim explains, "Ze'ev Jabotinsky was the first major Zionist leader to acknowledge that the Palestinians were a nation and that they could not be expected to renounce voluntarily their right to national self-determination."[8] Andrew Jackson never considered such a possibility vis-à-vis Native Americans. Jackson and Jabotinsky can be compared via their dishonesty, not their magnanimity.

Jabotinsky understood that Palestinians were not of a different species and would therefore have a typically human response to colonization: "Individual Arabs may perhaps be bought off but this hardly means that all the Arabs in Eretz Israel are willing to sell a patriotism that not even Papuans will trade. Every indigenous people will resist alien settlers as long as they see any hope of ridding themselves of the danger of foreign settlement."[9] His maxim about Indigenous people proved correct. Palestinians have vigorously resisted Israeli colonization for more than a century in ways both violent and nonviolent. Here is the major departure between Jackson and Jabotinsky. Jackson believed, or at least pretended to believe, that Natives were incapable of transitioning into productive nationhood (never mind millennia of evidence to the contrary); Jabotinsky, on the other hand, viewed the Palestinians, and Arabs more broadly, as competitors with the Yishuv (the pre-1948 Jewish settler community in Palestine) in a race to independent statehood. Jackson desired the eradication of the Natives because of their unsuitability for free-market capitalism; Jabotinsky considered the Arabs rational beings who must give way to a grander vision of Jewish habitation.

Yet Jabotinsky is not as far from Jackson as it might seem. Jabotinsky also believed in a national destiny, a benighted state in a Western image, free of the peculiar customs and concerns of the native inhabitants. His is a deeply Eurocentric conception of nationhood and modernity. Jabotinsky betrays his fundamental racism with the sneering observation that "not even Papuans" can be easily colonized. Never does Jabotinsky deem colonization a bad idea. It is impossible to proclaim respect for the person you endeavor to displace. For this reason, Jabotinsky professes a polite indifference to the Palestinians, but his assumptions render that profession disingenuous. In the end, Jabotinsky wanted to negatively alter their future.

The disingenuousness arises at the very start of "The Iron Wall":

> The author of these lines is considered to be an enemy of the Arabs, a proponent of their expulsion, etc. This is not true. My emotional relationship to the Arabs is the same as it is to all other peoples—polite indifference. My political relationship is characterized by two principles. First: the expulsion of the Arabs from Palestine is absolutely impossible in any form. There will always be two nations in Palestine—which is good enough for me, provided the Jews become the majority. Second: I am proud to have been a member of that group which formulated the Helsingfors Program. We formulated it, not only for Jews, but for all peoples, and its basis is the equality of all nations. I am prepared to swear, for us and our descendants, that we will never destroy this equality and we will never attempt to expel or oppress the Arabs. Our credo, as the reader can see, is completely peaceful. But it is absolutely another matter if it will be possible to achieve our peaceful aims through peaceful means. This depends, not on our relationship with the Arabs, but exclusively on the Arabs' relationship to Zionism.

Little evidence of Jabotinsky's organizing suggests that he was so devoted to practices of equality. He used a rhetorical flourish to conceal an ethnonationalism with no serious intention of coexistence. The Irgun militia Jabotinsky helped found played a prominent role in the displacement of Palestinians from 1947 to 1949.

These issues are straightforward. Of greater interest is Jabotinsky's normalization of Zionism as the standard of diplomacy. Jewish settlers are not responsible for the violence of their actions;

that onus belongs to the Palestinians. Jabotinsky thus attached imminence to Zionism. It arose from forces greater than the individual or collective. Its practice is an Arab concern. Settlement of Palestine is a by-product of Jewish selfhood; the Palestinian belongs to the category of "all other people." This genetic disparity provides the basis of Jabotinsky's vision of equality. Jabotinsky's argument is complex and artful: the Arabs will naturally be hostile to Zionism; that hostility justifies whatever violence accompanies the Zionist enterprise.

Jabotinsky never says what motivates his attachment to Zionism. His explanation is oblique: "We hold that Zionism is moral and just. And since it is moral and just, justice must be done. . . . There is no other morality." Jabotinsky's absolutist declaration underlies and therefore undermines his professions of humanism. Why is Zionism moral and just? Jabotinsky simply takes it as given, unworthy of serious exploration. In the framework of colonial discourses of self-determination through settlement and statehood, it was perfectly logical for Jabotinsky to leave the matter unexplored. Zionism is moral and just because it exists. To claim otherwise is to retard the course of progress. Settlement is not just a physical act, but an assumption of both ideology and identity. The hard-boiled realist Jabotinsky was also deeply messianic. Yet he was in no way ignorant of the historical dynamics he sought to rearrange. He refers to the Palestinians as "natives" and as "indigenous" and considers them a national community, going so far as to identify with their aspirations: "If it were possible (and I doubt this) to discuss Palestine with the Arabs of Baghdad and Mecca as if it were some kind of small, immaterial borderland, then Palestine would still remain for the Palestinians not a borderland, but their birthplace, the center and basis of their own national existence. Therefore it would be necessary to carry on colonization against the will of the Palestinian Arabs, which is the same condition that exists now."

The most quoted passage from "The Iron Wall" illuminates Jabotinsky's blend of blunt realism and messianic ardor:

> Thus we conclude that we cannot promise anything to the Arabs of the Land of Israel or the Arab countries. Their voluntary

agreement is out of the question. Hence those who hold that an agreement with the natives is an essential condition for Zionism can now say "no" and depart from Zionism. Zionist colonization, even the most restricted, must either be terminated or carried out in defiance of the will of the native population. This colonization can, therefore, continue and develop only under the protection of a force independent of the local population—an iron wall which the native population cannot break through. This is, in toto, our policy towards the Arabs. To formulate it any other way would only be hypocrisy.

Jabotinsky's metaphor almost sounds quaint in light of the apartheid wall Israel began erecting throughout the West Bank eighty-seven years later. Also notable is Jabotinsky's eager use of the word *colonization*; many of today's Zionists maintain that Israel is not a colonial state.

Jabotinsky used *colonization* because it encompasses the amalgamation of fantasy and audacity on which his argument relies. His prescriptions for Zionist colonization are forthright and, in their own context, reasonable: quit pretending that the natives will roll over and let you take their land; if you do not have the stomach for what this task requires, then join a movement of more suitable proclivity. Yet his moral absolutism about the necessity of colonization evokes a wide-ranging mythos of divinity and predestination. In these moments Jabotinsky bogs down in the folly of his realism. It compels him in the same argument to suggest promoting equality with the Palestinians and building a wall made of iron in order to sequester Arabs from Jews. Zionism has not since been able to reconcile these inherent contradictions. It is the destiny of all settler-colonial states to be fundamentally irrational. Settler-colonial states, however, accommodate contradiction in part by developing notions of rationality that render dispossession of Indigenous peoples a precondition for the existence of their progressive value systems. It is the sort of logic that compelled men like Jackson and Jabotinsky to consider it perfectly natural that natives need to be replaced.

In order to justify and naturalize his colonial ambitions, Jabotinsky turned to the conquest of America. It is a geography in which

numerous early Zionists found inspiration. Jabotinsky's discussion
of Natives is at once sloppy and shrewd:

> Every reader has some idea of the early history of other coun-
> tries which have been settled. I suggest that he recall all known
> instances. If he should attempt to seek but one instance of a
> country settled with the consent of those born there he will not
> succeed. The inhabitants (no matter whether they are civilized
> or savages) have always put up a stubborn fight. Furthermore,
> how the settler acted had no effect whatsoever. The Spaniards
> who conquered Mexico and Peru, or our own ancestors in the
> days of Joshua ben Nun behaved, one might say, like plunder-
> ers. But those "great explorers," the English, Scots and Dutch
> who were the first real pioneers of North America were people
> possessed of a very high ethical standard; people who not only
> wished to leave the redskins at peace but could also pity a fly;
> people who in all sincerity and innocence believed that in those
> virgin forests and vast plains ample space was available for
> both the white and red man. But the native resisted both bar-
> barian and civilized settler with the same degree of cruelty.

Analysts of Jabotinsky almost uniformly ignore the portions of "The
Iron Wall" dealing with American colonization. Such omissions
limit our understanding of both Jabotinsky and the political cultures
of modern Israel. Jabotinsky's delusion about the benign character
of Anglo settlement survives today in most iterations of U.S. patriotism; his insinuation that Zionism possesses the same innocent disposition has been fully endorsed by the arbiters of Israel's self-image.
The story of the settler of "a very high ethical standard" is apocryphal, but the greater misrepresentation exists in Jabotinsky's attenuated understanding of Native Americans. He deploys the evangelical
language of vast and virginal landscapes and recapitulates the conceits of coexistence and cooperation. But nowhere do actual Natives
figure into the analysis. Palestinians are equally absent.

Jabotinsky continues his example, which only becomes more
fantastical:

> Another point which had no effect at all was whether or not
> there existed a suspicion that the settler wished to remove the

inhabitant from his land. The vast areas of the U.S. never contained more than one or two million Indians. The inhabitants fought the white settlers not out of fear that they might be expropriated, but simply because there has never been an indigenous inhabitant anywhere or at any time who has ever accepted the settlement of others in his country. Any native people—it's all the same whether they are civilized or savage—views their country as their national home, of which they will always be the complete masters. They will not voluntarily allow, not only a new master, but even a new partner. And so it is for the Arabs.

Jabotinsky's pessimism—perhaps it can be called sobriety—about the unwillingness of the indigene to accept foreign settlement is warranted. It is also common wisdom to the point of truism. No native population accepts its own dispossession, but this point is not where emphasis should be. No would-be colonizer sets out to control a new territory with the purpose of implementing equal rights. When a realist like Jabotinsky acknowledges the recalcitrant native, then, he also supplements honesty with deceit. The native's reaction to the colonial encounter does not need to be explained; the onus of explanation belongs to the settler. Jabotinsky, like Jackson, explains nothing concrete; they merely recite the high-minded platitudes of settler zealotry.

Colonization inevitably relies on mythologized histories, but even by this standard Jabotinsky deeply misunderstands U.S. settlement. This misunderstanding illustrates how the colonizer's need to envision a new future requires him to invent a new past. The Indigenous population of what is now the United States was quite a bit larger than one or two million. Estimates vary, but some put the number as high as fifteen million, with most counts ranging between five and nine million. It is true that in Jabotinsky's time such studies had not been conducted, but Jabotinsky did not seek scientific accuracy. He was rhetorically invested in the mythology of an empty landscape. Colonial narratives have little to do with illuminating historical nuance; they are artful re-creations of the world that coerce inculcation into settler common sense. In fact,

Jabotinsky's discourse is notably ahistorical. He makes the stunning claim that the Indians "fought the white settlers not out of fear that they might be expropriated." They resisted settlement, according to Jabotinsky, simply because that is what happens. (To Jabotinsky, the same is true of colonization: it just happens.) In this schema, conflict becomes a primordial rather than rational reaction. Foreign aggression is not the reason for resistance; rather, some vague form of atavism is the culprit.

He completes his thoughts on American colonization with this appeal: "We can talk as much as we want about our good intentions; but [the Palestinians] understand as well as we what is not good for them. They look upon Palestine with the same instinctive love and true fervor that any Aztec looked upon his Mexico or any Sioux looked upon his prairie. To think that the Arabs will voluntarily consent to the realization of Zionism in return for the cultural and economic benefits we can bestow on them is infantile." The words *instinctive* and *fervor* give insight into Jabotinsky's mentality. I have attempted to illustrate that his crude realism does not represent the extent to which he reiterates typically messianic and deterministic narratives deployed by forebears like Andrew Jackson. Here Jabotinsky makes that reiteration more explicit. Few things about the native are rational. Even when his actions can be explained by logic, the motivations for those actions are shrouded in some unknowable element of their innate character.

Jabotinsky is not always so oblique, though, as when he reprises the civilized/savage binary: "Culturally [the Arabs] are 500 years behind us, spiritually they do not have our endurance or our strength of will, but this exhausts all of the internal differences." Jabotinsky's list of internal differences is not very long, but those he mentions are significant—to the point of exhausting every imaginable dissimilarity. In a short essay filled with memorable lines, this one stands out. It is the moment at which Jabotinsky appears to lose control of his cool, efficient rhetoric. After spending much time convincing the reader that the need to sequester Palestinians from Jews is nothing personal, he confesses that, despite his seemingly disinterested assessment, he believes the Arabs to in fact be inferior. It would be difficult, perhaps impossible, for Jabotinsky to put forward his recommendations in the absence of that belief. Once he theorizes a civilizational discrepancy between Jew and Arab, the reader can partake of her own form of revisionism, one in which, upon a reread, Jabotinsky's inscrutable gaps of logic suddenly make sense.

Much that Jabotinsky proposes is contingent on the mythical figure of the Native. Whenever we speak of a connection between Natives and Palestinians, we suggest that particular historical conditions bring them into contact. Jabotinsky articulates those conditions. The primary condition is a disparity of power between colonizer and colonized, complemented by a standard array of messianic narratives rationalizing that disparity as natural. Another important condition is the centrality of homelands to Native and Palestinian identities and the corresponding devaluation of the land by the settlers and their military apparatuses. Jabotinsky's temporal sequencing is interesting: he puts a five hundred-year gap between the Jew and the Arab. It may be an arbitrary number, or it may allude to the time that has passed since the age of European exploration. Either way, it situates the Palestinian in the same premodern category as the Native, the Aborigine, and the African.

Yet the Native foregrounds the Palestinian. It is with reference to American conquest that Jabotinsky attempts to make moral and political sense of Zionism. Jabotinsky did not desire to re-create a history but to extend it and apply it to a new geography. The British and French may have led the way in the Levant, but the United States had provided a more useful blueprint, one with a much greater sense of purpose and permanence. Jabotinsky sought to reproduce that blueprint, which could occur only through force and coercion. The militia he founded was based on the stark realism of Native American resistance. He knew how the Palestinians would react to Zionism because he saw how Natives reacted to the European settlement he endeavored to rejuvenate.

Vis-à-vis the Zionist colonization of Palestine, then, hundreds of years of prior context exist. Leaders such as Jabotinsky and David Ben-Gurion, Israel's founding prime minister, recognized the importance of that context in both formulating a vision of state building and deploying a lofty rhetoric of national achievement. Those interested in decolonizing America and Palestine might find a similar usefulness, albeit for a more ethical purpose. It is not enough simply to reference the genocide of Natives as an abstract backdrop to Israeli colonialism; nor is it adequate to invoke that genocide without a concomitant engagement with its ongoing effects. The colonizer on both continents presumed to know the natives in the same way, as a function of his own grandiose desires and nebulous self-image. The advocate for Palestine on American soil necessarily has a vexing relationship with these histories, but she will have a hard time clarifying her role as an off-site practitioner of decolonization in the Arab world unless she attempts to become an on-site practitioner of decolonization in the United States and Canada.

Nothing better illuminates the transactional nature of colonization than Jabotinsky's reflections on the American Indian. Unlike many contemporaries, he assiduously positioned Indians within rather than beyond history, but the history into which he positioned them was wholly mythological. He recapitulated typical narratives of the Indian, but he is not simply mimetic. He evokes ideas and traditions that inform his typology of the savage. These ideas and traditions allow him to speculate that Natives have agency, but do nothing, or very little, to alter the underlying logic of land appropriation. No matter how diligently the Native would resist, America had to come into being. In Jabotinsky's mind, the colonial imperative is even more natural than the resistance inscribed in Native DNA. That he had little understanding of Natives or their political complexities only adds verisimilitude to his unshakable confidence.

"The Iron Wall" is a fascinating bit of political writing. Jabotinsky's staid pragmatism is reminiscent of Henry Kissinger and other proponents of realpolitik, but, upon close analysis, he sounds like no American so much as Andrew Jackson. For Jackson, it was a given that Natives had to be removed. He never offered a concrete reason, only messianic abstractions that relied on a set of shared assumptions with his audience about settler civility. The Native was bound for extinction—not because of American aggression, but because of the vicissitudes of a glorious civilizational trajectory. Jabotinsky picked up this idea and applied it to his idealized version of the Israeli future. His arguments are so compelling in part because of the certainty they evince about a particular order in the world, which demystifies the Palestinian while simultaneously eulogizing Palestine. Jabotinsky speculated that the Palestinian would resist Zionism for perfectly valid reasons. None of those reasons, however, was more valid than the need to colonize Palestine. The Palestinian, no matter how human her actions, will always antedate history by five centuries.

The Mysteries of Reason

The differences between Jackson's and Jabotinsky's discourses are largely cosmetic. They share profound connections of desire and outlook, though not of style or temperament. Let us recap a few of those connections:

- Both men blame Indigenous peoples for their dispossession. Jackson and Jabotinsky proffer that blame not necessarily because of Indigenous strategic blunders or immorality. Indeed, both articulate sympathy for the indigene, though not compassion, which indicates that the sympathy is a rhetorical tactic. (It is difficult, in any case, to be fully sympathetic to those one aims to displace.) The indigenes are responsible for their own dispossession because the colonizer is incapable of accepting responsibility for his behavior, which is not an act of agency but a fulfillment of grand historical forces.

- Both men ascribe an unchanging, innate disposition to the indigene. Jackson and Jabotinsky do not position Indigenous peoples beyond history—their determination to expel Indigenous peoples in order to enact their own histories makes this clear—but they view them as unable to progress through history's linear continuum. As a result, Indigenous peoples are unfit for modernity.

- Both men proclaim an inability to comprehend the indigene. They are confident in their ability to understand the indigene's behavior, and to predict his actions and reactions, but the indigene's unchanging, innate disposition is incomprehensible. To know the indigene's motivations is to forfeit access to civility. Neither Jackson nor Jabotinsky explores why Indigenous peoples behave the way they do (as imagined by Jackson and Jabotinsky); they treat that behavior as an ahistorical given instead. Nearly all iterations of settler colonization possess this feature. The colonizer rarely engages the cultural and philosophical complexities of the native. He does so to the extent that he contemplates the metaphysics of flora and fauna.

- Both men profess a deep commitment to reason but tacitly rely on messianism and mythology. Settler-colonial logic is inherently restricted to the psychology of the conqueror. There is little ability, or craving, for any self-reflection that moves beyond the repetitive desire for nationalistic actualization. Their secular interventions thus embody a divine mandate.

- Both men accept the necessity of violence in generating modernity. The national enlightenment Jackson and Jabotinsky seek requires bloodshed and displacement. Human beings must be uprooted in order for democracy to prevail. The modern, in these instances, is a form of tribal violence revised by the language of civility. The civilizational glories Jackson and Jabotinsky seek are brutal. The spilling of blood foregrounds the creation of a new man, who emerges from the majesty of conflict. His character is built on the grandeur of the gun and the splendor of battle. Violence presupposes historical triumph.

- Both men treat mythology as unimpeachable. By "mythology," I refer (in this case) to histories developed in the colonizer's self-image and subsequently interpreted as empirical or authentic. Jackson and Jabotinsky consider it imperative to act on those histories. Historical mythology, then, is incomplete until it can be enacted by the same

agents responsible for its invention. Indigenous peoples
lack comparable histories. Indigenous history exists only
in fantasies of the settler's future.

Connecting Jackson and Jabotinsky to inter/nationalism is not trenchant. To understand them in light of decolonization first requires
a recovery of the indigene absent yet constantly visible in their
discourses. We might recover the indigene by locating her in the
assumptions that comprise the basis of my comparison.

Indigenous peoples are critical to Jackson's and Jabotinsky's
sense of ontology, yet those Indigenous peoples are not sentient
beings, but inventions of Jackson's and Jabotinsky's imaginations.
Jabotinsky comes much closer to theorizing an Indigenous consciousness than does Jackson, but he never fully engages Palestinians beyond the set of traits he also recognizes in Jews. The settler
must invent the indigene before inventing himself. Any project of
foreign settlement necessitates the deployment of new histories as
portals onto the present and presuppositions of the future. This
sort of project also necessitates theories of disparate personhood
and agency: the temporal gaps in civilizational development represent apertures that the settler wishes to eliminate in favor of a
triumphalist, linear society. The native produces incoherence. The
settler craves order. Society cannot be ordered in a primitive state.

Jackson and Jabotinsky are fully discrete but mutually constitutive. This relationship is possible because both men habituate a
political space in constant dialogue with the mysticism of state
building. Such an observation is not to imply that the material conditions Jackson and Jabotinsky inhabited were identical. The circumstances of their colonial projects differ significantly, but their
worldviews are in conversation across temporal and geographic
restrictions.

It is nonetheless productive to highlight some of these differing circumstances. Indian removal and the *nakba* both entailed violent and involuntary removal of Indigenous populations from their
ancestral land bases so that colonists could make space for increased
settlement and avail themselves of natural resources and an im-
proved geostrategic position. Both acts were justified by the need

for a higher order of human society to prevail. And both validated the role of violence in the development and maintenance of Western modernity. Yet removal can be considered the grander event. It involved dozens of Native nations (though five of them—the Cherokee, Choctaw, Chickasaw, Creek, and Seminole—are most often associated with it). It also occurred over a longer period of time, though one might argue convincingly that both removal and the *nakba* are ongoing. To be clearer, the time frame of the actual physical removal of Indigenous peoples was longer in the U.S. Southeast than in Palestine.

Another notable difference is the fact that removal was a legislative act, debated for years on the floor of Congress. The *nakba* too developed from years of planning, but that planning was largely covert or extralegal. The sitting president of the United States lobbied for removal and produced grandiloquent justifications for the Removal Act. The landscape on which removal was to happen traversed thousands of miles, in contrast to Palestine's thin geographic profile. In the end, the soldiers who enforced removal, throughout different moments of the same era, were obeying a legal dictate that preceded the creation of international law. The Yishuv, followed by the Israelis, carried out the *nakba* in defiance of United Nations jurisdiction and according to a strategic calculus at odds with the majority of their public pronouncements. As they planned a widespread displacement of Palestinians behind closed doors, mainly under the guise of Plan Dalet, Yishuv leaders assured the UN and Western powers that they were content to accept the conceptual borders of partition, which were much smaller than the territory they intended to conquer in collusion with Arab elites, among them Abdullah I, the king of Transjordan.[10] No such treachery existed with Jackson and other champions of the Removal Act.

Despite these and other differences, the discursive foundations of removal and the *nakba*, as exemplified by Jackson and Jabotinsky, are striking in their reliance on the same narrow mythos of progress, which constitutes the very existence of the settler. This mythos, even in its secular incarnations, is fundamentally biblical: the settler is aggrieved, usually escaping persecution in the originating nation, and must be redeemed through a violent national rebirth. Natives and Palestinians end up in the same category of dispossession simply by existing. They remain antagonists in the hawkish narratives central to the identities of the United States and Israel. Linking their decolonial struggles, then, need not rehash the messianism of the conqueror. As Blackfeet lawyer Gyasi Ross notes, "[My] fraternal feeling for my brothers and sisters in Gaza and on the West Bank is due to a much more basic and primal feeling of fear: the realization that what befalls one oppressed group inevitably befalls others."[11]

Ross broadens his analysis while keeping sight of the mutual conditions he earlier identifies:

> Indigenous people, as well as other oppressed groups world-wide, regardless of race or religion, have a vested interest in learning from the genocidal atrocities that the U.S. government initiated on Native Americans. Every person who strives for humanity also has a strong interest in preventing those same atrocities from occurring in another place at another time to another group of people—in this particular situation, to the Palestinians.[12]

This point, increasingly common among Native writers and activists, removes colonization from the realm of the mystical and assesses it as a material reality. Ross treats the conquest of America as a foundational event from which other acts of displacement emerge, including the Zionist colonization of Palestine. Those who occupy the continent thus have an impetus to contextualize overseas settlement with the American prototype.

Walter Mignolo theorizes these phenomena in ways that illuminate the philosophical grounding of Jackson and Jabotinsky:

> Modernity is, for many (for Jürgen Habermas or Charles Taylor) an essentially or exclusively European phenomenon. In these lectures, I will argue that modernity is, in fact, a European phenomenon but one constituted in a dialectical relation with a non-European alterity that is its ultimate content. Modernity appears when Europe affirms itself as the "center" of a World

History that it inaugurates: the "periphery" that surrounds this center is consequently part of its self-definition. The occlusion of this periphery (and of the role of Spain and Portugal in the formation of the modern world system from the late fifteenth to the mid-seventeenth centuries) leads the major contemporary thinkers of the "center" into a Eurocentric fallacy in their understanding of modernity. If their understanding of the genealogy of modernity is thus partial and provincial, their attempts at a critique or defense of it are likewise unilateral and, in part, false.[13]

Mignolo works from a notion of "de-linking," a theoretical paradigm similar to inter/nationalism despite the apparent disparities of their nomenclature. De-linking does not refer to Indigenous communities involved in the work of decolonization, but to the monopolization by the colonizer of normative definitions of democracy and modernity. Mignolo suggests a de-linking of colonial logic from the fantasies of equality and liberation. He assesses this problem by alluding to a messianic dreamscape:

Under the spell of neo-liberalism and the magic of the media promoting it, modernity and modernization, together with democracy, are being sold as a package trip to the promised land of happiness, a paradise where, for example, when you can no longer buy land because land itself is limited and not producible or monopolized by those who control the concentration of wealth, you can buy virtual land!! Yet, when people do not buy the package willingly or have other ideas of how economy and society should be organized, they become subject to all kinds of direct and indirect violence. It is not a spiritual claim, or merely a spiritual claim that I am making. The crooked rhetoric that naturalizes "modernity" as a universal global process and point of arrival hides its darker side, the constant reproduction of "coloniality."[14]

This "constant reproduction of 'coloniality'" is evident whenever Jackson or Jabotinsky deify settlement and displacement, treating them as triumphs of human ingenuity. Mignolo's invocation of marketing—"the package"—is an apt description for the sort of rhetoric that conceptualizes Native dispossession as a gift or obligation. It creates a new country from the savage entrails of a primitive geography.

Building from Mignolo's analysis, and using a comparison of Jackson and Jabotinsky as a framework, I am interested in inter/ nationalism not simply as a mode of comparison that bridges temporal discrepancies, but as an insight into a universal logic of capitalism in relation to foreign conquest. That Jackson and Jabotinsky were active in different centuries is less important than their maintenance (or creation) of a timeless narrative, which allowed them to often sound the same despite temporal and geographic disparities. We see engagement with this timeless narrative in decolonial communities. For example, Erica Violet Lee, a leader in the Idle No More movement, says,

> For Indigenous people of Turtle Island, supporting the Palestinian struggle is of significance. We know what it is to be denied our right to life by colonizers who could not see our humanity; those who only viewed our bodies as obstacles to possessing the land and its resources. In solidarity, Native Americans work to prevent the loss of Palestinian homelands, because we recognize that what is occurring is not just a loss of land, but an erasure of our knowledge, our history and our ancestors. We must stand up for people under colonial occupation to assert their sovereignty and dream of lives without the ever-present fear of death.[15]

Lee's argument is experiential, but seeks to understand the colonization of America as an ongoing process beyond the borders of the United States and Canada. Her analysis of the body as obstacle highlights a messianic impulse to possession. The colonizer seeks to possess the land and resources of the native, but also the means by which the native can be possessed of agency. Property extends well beyond acreage and real-estate documents. It also encompasses states of being. Indigenous peoples can become products of colonial ownership, just as they can reinvent geography as a dynamic element of an itinerant existence.

The discourses of mutual American and Israeli exceptionality are under more scrutiny in inter/national spaces because it is difficult to overlook their inveterate usage among commenters and politicians. Indeed, those discourses are essential to America's plutocratic governance. Here is White House press secretary Josh Earnest in 2014 after a minor furor arose around Barack Obama's tepid criticism of Israel's aggressive settlement of the West Bank: "The fact is, when it comes to American values, it's American values that lend this country's unwavering support to Israel. It's American values that have led us to fight for and secure funding to strengthen Israel's security in tangible ways."[16] The first notable thing about Earnest's quote is its fawning, plaintive tone. We see an earnest retreat from criticism and an assumption of abject sycophancy; the special relationship is inscrutable, akin, at times, to the salvation of something sacred.

The quote is worthy of close reading, though. Earnest does not invoke geostrategic interests, the normal tactic of policy makers. Instead, he focuses on values, whose appeals to emotion offer concrete sources of affinity. Values are fungible, but I see no reason to disagree with Earnest's proclamations. The values he exalts have been practically unchanged for centuries, one reason why Israeli Prime Minister Binyamin Netanyahu could so effortlessly recite them in order to produce the effect of a dog whistle: "It's against the American values. And it doesn't bode well for peace." Netanyahu references U.S. government criticism of Israel's announcement of new settlement construction. That criticism was pyrrhic, but the performance requires a reaffirmation of shared values. Earnest quickly obliged, attaching those values to militarism, their inevitable origin and stopping point: "It's American values that have led us to fund and build an Iron Dome system that protected the lives of countless innocent Israeli citizens." In this exchange about values, the conflict is not about contradictory values, but about who can most loudly trumpet the values of alliance.

The American values precede Israel's, an important feature of this dialogue. The obvious explanation is that American conquest occurred before Jewish Zionism, but an even earlier taproot accounts for the transatlantic identification so embraced by American and

Israeli politicians (and the populations they nominally represent). Foreign settlement necessarily emerges from mythology; American and Israeli settlement share a common origin myth, biblical stories of violent salvation and a glorious predestination. Earnest's valorization of shared American and Israeli values, then, is consummately messianic, though it is doubtful either he or the majority of his audience would read it that way. The messianism is informed by and entangled with various points of injustice. To return to Mike Krebs and Dana Olwan's analysis of the indispensability of racism and sexual violence to colonization, it is critical to attach the abstract connotation of values to the violent practices they engender. Only in doing so can we understand what these values actually mean to those who deploy them and to those who suffer their deployment.

Glen Coulthard offers a useful critique of colonial values in transit by appealing to place-based notions of universal justice, raising questions of an "ethical responsibility to support other struggles that stems from our reciprocal relationship to the land." On notions of inter/nationalism, he says, "Solidarity must be a reciprocal relationship and this demands that Indigenous peoples be more open to and take up other communities' struggles more seriously."[17] Many new modes of theorization in Native and Indigenous studies emphasize engagement with global practices of neoliberalism and the structural iniquities they sustain. If we consider how derivative of one another colonial discourses in the United States and Israel can be, an imperative to what Coulthard calls solidarity seems self-evident. The process is not so trenchant in reality. It requires, as Coulthard and others note, constant reference to the historical dynamics of settlement and their effects on the present configuration of nation-states. Jackson and Jabotinsky are as much a part of today's colonial violence as they were when alive to foment dispossession.

A reciprocal solidarity should arise from whatever location we occupy. By "location," I refer to numerous concomitant phenomena: our ancestral lands, ethical commitments, spiritual/religious/ceremonial practices, viewpoints, worldviews, aspirations, and anxieties. In short, the histories we inherit by virtue of our ancestors' locations are the impetus to seek community among those with different inherited histories, though these histories share the power of inheritance. We have to treat our gestures of solidarity carefully in order that they do not become encroachment. When Muscogee poet Joy Harjo, for instance, violated the BDS call by reading and accepting a fellowship at Tel Aviv University, a serious, sometimes acrimonious debate occurred. The debate illuminated both the usefulness and the pitfalls of Native–Palestinian solidarity.

I could write at length of the complexities of Harjo's decision and the ensuing conversations, but I am mostly interested in a particular response by Palestine solidarity activists. The response highlights how solidarity, even when undertaken in good faith, can fall short of its own ideals. It also reveals how Natives and Palestinians remain encumbered by the set of political and philosophical imperatives so starkly articulated by Jackson and Jabotinsky. In the interest of greater context, I offer a few general remarks: I was one of Harjo's critics, though I preferred to register my objections in private conversation (with colleagues; I have never spoken with Harjo). Harjo seemed quite surprised by the reaction her choices generated, though in the end she refused to back away from them. Contrary to the belief that Palestinians initially confronted Harjo, it was Robert Warrior and J. Kēhaulani Kauanui who first approached her to cancel. Harjo added a trip to the West Bank to her itinerary and spoke of her sense of community with the Palestinians under occupation. Although Harjo's actions brought Native–Palestinian solidarity into closer communion, it also created some tension among Natives and Palestinians, as well as among Natives themselves.

I am curious about the emergence of the phrase "the Palestinian Trail of Tears," which a number of anti-Zionist commenters employed to describe what they viewed as Harjo's betrayal. While I would consider Harjo's decision a betrayal of sorts, particularly vis-à-vis the Natives who implored her to cancel, I find the "Palestinian Trail of Tears" formulation troublesome in its wording and substance. The wording intimates a possessive investment by Palestinians in the Trail of Tears, which subsumes it to a different set of historical circumstances devoid of Native agency. In terms of its substance, it tacitly implicates Harjo in a genocide carried out by the U.S. government against her ancestors. I consider Harjo's trip ill-considered at best and hostile at worst, but to lay responsibility on her for a trail of tears, even one that occurred in Palestine, complicates rather than clarifies the conditions of inter/nationalism. I suggest a more historicized approach to solidarity, one that meticulously identifies the various assumptions that regulate liberatory discourses. It happens often, and indeed occurred during the Harjo controversy, but I caution Palestine solidarity activists against inadvertently (or purposefully, if that is the case) limiting Natives to the referents of a Palestinian symbology.

I do not raise this critique to be combative. I reiterate that most of the discussion around Harjo's Tel Aviv visit was productive and sophisticated. In the "Palestinian Trail of Tears" formulation, I see a good example of where folks interested in developing inter/national communities can more carefully approach the subjects of their concern. The formulation is instructive in light of Jabotinsky's misreading of American history. (Perhaps it would be more accurate to say that Jabotinsky accurately read a mythologized incarnation of American history.) Jabotinsky recycled the American colonial logic that Jackson helped consecrate. The Trail of Tears, then, becomes another iconic example of history mediated through endless retellings of myth. It is better to critically reinterpret narratives than it is to reinvent their verisimilitude. Palestinians could have referenced to better effect the Trail of Tears as it happened on its own geography. It perfectly foretold what would become of Zionist colonization.

Conclusion: Iron Deficiency

Iron is essential to our survival. It inhabits a protein that carries oxygen to our extremities. Perhaps Jabotinsky did not use the term only metaphorically. His exaltations of strength and steadfastness, after all, sharply contrast nearly all the connotations of anemia. The body of the Israeli state could not survive without this self-regenerating chemical.

Jackson was in no way afflicted by political anemia. He browbeat rather than shepherded the Indian Removal Act into existence.

He oversaw its implementation with brutal proficiency. In such vast geography, Jackson had no need for iron walls, only huge swaths of territory to insulate the Native from American progress. It would help the Indians, he claimed, but he never took a moment to examine the bloody contradictions of his altruism.

Yet no barricade or hinterland can separate the indigene from her homeland. Territory accompanies people across iron barriers and foreign landscapes. No colonizer can build a wall high or strong enough to separate a people from its own history. Nor can settlers fully remove a people from the land of its ancestors, even when the land falls under settler control. Indigenous peoples are capable of imagining territory as a distinctive element of their place in the world. Most settlers conceptualize land as an accoutrement to an imagined cultural supremacy.

By comparing Jackson and Jabotinsky I have attempted to illustrate how we can productively situate inter/nationalism in close analysis of a shared set of colonial ideals. Those ideals profess grandeur but in reality are tenuous and hermetic. We have terrific opportunities, then, to continue dismantling the predestined narratives of civility and progress. This opportunity, in turn, enables us to more rigorously undertake decolonial analysis. It also makes such a task easier. U.S. and Israeli leaders constantly deify a "special relationship," but exploring the conditions of the relationship makes it clear that the relationship is constructed of pixie dust and delusion. The colonizer knows full well to whom the land belongs. His constant professions of godly obligation all but prove it.

4.
INTER/NATIONAL AESTHETICS
Palestinians in Native Poetry

◾   ◾   ◾

Literary criticism may appear a bit out of place in this book, but I contend that analysis of cultural production is necessary to decolonization. In that spirit, I would like to examine how Natives and Palestinians interact in literature, and in poetry specifically. Through this genre, we access infinite ways of imagining ourselves, and one another, both symbolically and concretely. I adhere to no particular critical tradition, having decided some time ago that an interesting reading need not observe a methodological formula (which I suppose makes me an unwitting poststructuralist, minus the adjective "interesting"). My aim is not simply to interpret, though; I want to highlight the uses of Palestine and Palestinians in Native poetry (that written by the Indigenous peoples of North America). The theme of Palestine in this poetry offers wonderful forms of inter/national engagement. Reading the poetry itself constitutes an inter/national practice.

Plenty of Palestinians have invoked Natives in their poetry (and in other genres), but I want to center the Native author here—and in so doing examine Palestine as a theme outside its own physical geography (but still very much within that geography). I thus consider this chapter to be an example of Native literary criticism, for I explore Native work with emphasis on a particular theme, that of Palestine. That is to say, I do not want the theme to supersede the context or content. As far as I know, nobody has yet systematically explored how Native poets treat Palestine in their work, be it as an identity, a political space, a metaphor, an emblem, a prototype, or an inspiration. This attempt is thus simultaneously daunting and exciting (if not from the reader's point of view, then certainly from mine). I will consider it well worth the labor if others take a moment to extend or revise what I manage to produce.

In selecting what I consider to be a broad cross section of poetry (nationally, geographically, stylistically, and generically) I underscore coverage rather than detailed critique of a single author. While I attempt to proffer analysis that does more than synopsize, I am keen on a set of thematic relationships that emerge across nations and so I will highlight a particular aesthetic used by various poets. Certain features of this aesthetic are visible:

- Native poets do not mention Palestine as an abstract space detached from their own ancestral grounds. They instead treat it as a component of their own political identities.

- Native poets view Palestine as integral to global projects of liberation. Palestine thus conjoins the Third and Fourth Worlds.

- In Native poetry, Palestine often exists in a historical continuum that dislodges it from the Arab world and originates its modern condition in North America.

- In Native poetry, Palestine is a place of great suffering, and thus worthy of great empathy.

- Native poets center the humanity of Palestinians rather than condemning Israel from the point of view of Jewish dissenters. This distinction is important, as it illustrates an investment in Palestine as the site of provenance, thereby displacing Israel from its typical originary position.

- There is often a sense of reinvigoration of Native decolonial struggle through reference to or engagement with Palestine. In some cases, Palestine becomes a site of renewal, evoking a biblical imagery. Such imagery might appear to reinforce settler mythology, but in reality it undermines that mythology by revising scriptural narratives of Indigeneity.

- Native poets connect Palestinian suffering to U.S. (and Canadian) policy. Rather than naming policy merely as imperialistic, they conceptualize it as an extension of North American colonial practices.

- In Native poetry, Palestine is not usually isolated, but mentioned in the context of corporate malfeasance, the carceral state, police violence, upheaval in the Southern Hemisphere, class iniquity, and so forth. One might say that Palestine appears in the presence of political poetry, but I am wary of categories, particularly those that specify something that is actually universal.

Some Native poets have spoken about Palestine beyond the form of verse, which gives us a better sense of their reasoning around its inclusion in their work. (I take the naive view, at least in this case, that authors are useful authorities on their own writing.) Salish and Cree writer and activist Lee Maracle, for example, proclaims:

It does not take too much historical digging to find out that Israel is the newest colonizing settler state in the world, that it displaced several million Palestinians, corralled them into refugee camps and denied them the [most basic] of human rights. Hunger, displacement from their homelands and lack of medical care all dog the Palestinian people: the original citizens of Palestine. Canada was a gift from Britain to the white male settlers of Canada who cleared the land, killed the Indians and Buffalo in exactly the same way that Israel [a gift from the United States and Britain to the European Jews] has cleared the land of Palestinians, expropriated their villages, farms and murdered all those who resist. Both settler populations had an obligation to dispossess and oppress the Indigenous people to maintain the settler regime.[1]

Maracle synthesizes nearly the complete array of poetic interventions into Palestine. She positions Israel as a new incarnation of an old phenomenon. She alludes to the messianic notion of land as a commodity to be gifted by a higher authority. She explicitly connects U.S./Canadian and Israeli colonization, treating them as essentially identical. She applies the modern notion of human rights to the crimes of early settlers in the United States and Canada, thus collapsing temporal legal distinctions. And she centers the indigene as steward of the land, rather than as an impediment to progress or rapprochement.

Erica Violet Lee, a Cree, raises slightly different concerns, though in the same broad context that animates Maracle:

> Lately, I find myself frustrated by the way that women's voices are still routinely silenced within activist circles on issues that directly affect us, and the gendered nature of roles we are pushed into during organizing (read: the background). This is certainly the case with Indigenous women and Palestinian women who work tirelessly at resistance, only to have our contributions undervalued and silenced; to be called divisive when we raise issues of patriarchy and misogyny.[2]

Lee points to issues of marginalization within solidarity communities, themes that poets of color have long explored. By looking inward at the problems of activist communities, she performs a central function of decolonization, sustained critique of how injustice can be reproduced among the colonized. She challenges tidy notions of dichotomized oppression, pointing out that internalized forms of colonial violence reproduce themselves in Indigenous communities without constant self-reflection. Her focus is on the liberation of Indigenous peoples; her criticism thus complements Maracle's, though she employs a slightly different approach.

These concerns turn up in the poetry I assess. I am wary of criticism that solely (or mainly) attempts to identify sociopolitical phenomena in creative writing. I prefer to highlight thematic connections across a relatively wide range of work. As a result, I treat Palestine as an aesthetic in Native poetry, not simply a site of political engagement. We can examine Palestine in Native poetry the same way we assess the symbolism of the color green or the allegorical characteristics of a ceremonial outfit: not as an exhaustive indicator of finite value but as an ongoing conversation, open-ended and ambiguous and self-reflective. The consistent device in this open-endedness and ambiguity and self-reflection is that, in the hands of Native poets, Palestine always becomes Indian country.

I only discuss one Palestinian poet, Mahmoud Darwish, though many writers of Palestinian origin produce what might be called "Indian" themes. This chapter offers a complement to my discussion of how Palestine became important to American Indian studies. In this case, I examine cultural production to see how Palestine can be deterritorialized from its physical geography and in turn evolve into a type of inter/national symbology while remaining grounded in its own unique space. I then consider how that symbology both emerges from and informs creative dynamics (and dynamic creativity) in Native poetry. Darwish abets this methodology because his famous poem "The 'Red Indian's' Penultimate Speech to the White Man" inspired a response by Lakota activist, actor, and politician Russell Means. This interchange presents an opportunity to assess a concrete example of inter/national poetic symbolism.

By considering young and old poets, different forms (including song lyrics), and a range of tribal, gender, cultural, and sexual identities, I hope to have compiled enough material to assess the transit of themes across a broad geography (spatial and metaphorical). In addition to Darwish/Means, Lee Maracle, and Erica Violet Lee, I critique poems by John Trudell (Santee Dakota), Carter Revard (Osage), and Edgar Gabriel Silex (Pueblo).

Erica Violet Lee:
Women as the Consciousness of Decolonization

In an untitled poem delivered at a 2014 Saskatoon rally in support of Gaza, Lee wastes no time staking connections between Native and Palestinian women. Beginning with the second stanza, the reader encounters a list of juxtapositions:

> We both live in occupied territories
> But what can I know about you
> Half a world away from me
>
> You and me, we know violence
> The pain of our mothers
> The memories of this land
>
> We share a history of being moved
> Removed
> moved again
> taken from our homes
> and wondering if we'll ever go back[3]

Lee simultaneously questions and affirms the ability of Indigenous women to "know" each other across political and cultural boundaries. Yet her cardinal line, "what can I know about you," finishes without a question mark. The inquiry thus becomes declarative. It is a statement filled with confidence while feigning doubt. Knowing one another, then, need not occur simply through the conditions of the present; it also happens based on a common understanding of the past.

Lee positions women as the consciousness and muscle of decolonization. Her poem illuminates the ways in which Native and Palestinian women endure the double burden of colonial violence and the adoption of its violent practices within their own communities. She makes clear who embodies spiritual and material responsibilities:

> —You and me
> We're the nation
>
> And this is for the mothers and daughters
> leading movements from Gaza to the grasslands
>
> —You and me
> We're the resistance

Lee renders *nation* and *resistance* coterminous through a repetitive grammar. She outfits both with the same article, *the,* and an identical, isolated line sequence. She also deploys the pronoun *we* as the subject of both nouns, which refers to Indigenous women. The reference is clear in the lines "And this is for the mothers and daughters / leading movements from Gaza to the grasslands."

The pronoun *we* can initially be read as inclusive, but it is specific to particular demographics. Yet its specificity is universal. This universality is not an example of verbal irony but a philosophical observation that woman constitutes the nation's essential characteristics. Lee does not reduce Indigenous resistance to women; she highlights the necessary role of women in effective decolonization. Women must be present in all constituent parts of the Indigenous nation. The basis of this belief is not Lee's desire for exclusion but acknowledgment of the ways in which gender exclusivity has come to affect colonized societies:

> This is for the women who never left their houses
> until the day they were carried out
>
> —Tell me again about your revolution
>
> This is for the women who are raped
> and told that speaking out will dishonor their community
> and abortion is a crime
> So it's best to suffer in silence
>
> —Tell me again about your damn revolution

In such conditions, the revolution is damned. It is a matter of dignity in addition to one of freedom: "And we won't fight only to return home as servants." Lee identifies decolonial activism as incomplete. Its incompleteness is illuminated in spatial restrictions: home confinement and a lack of access to adequate medical care. The restrictions are also verbal (perhaps, by extension, emotional): speaking against violence within Native communities is verboten, itself a violent restriction of personhood. Lee's reconfiguration of the line "Tell me again about your damn revolution" by adding *damn* to modify revolution illuminates a frustration that emerges in real time as the narrative develops. The naming of oppression enacts the passionate revision of an extant irritation.

Lee ends the poem with the same structural rhythm:

— You and me
We're the resistance

And this is for the women
who are told not to speak
not to write or read
not to dream or feel
but do it anyway

— You and me
We're the revolution

Her use of pronouns in this excerpt, as throughout the poem, is noteworthy. The second-person *you* appears to be universal, while the first-person *me* intimates the author's presence as a character. Close reading disrupts this assumption, though. Lee conflates the tenses by integrating herself into the audience she addresses, thus transforming her from a character to an embodiment of a revolution that is both symbolic and overt.

Lee anchors her revolutionary impulses in the figures of Amal, Einav, and Anna Mae Aquash. An Israeli soldier shot Amal, a Palestinian teenager, while she was reading a book; the same soldier killed his girlfriend Einav two years later. Aquash was an American Indian Movement (AIM) activist executed, most likely by other AIM members, on the Pine Ridge Reservation in South Dakota during a period of heavy FBI infiltration. The common thread in their stories is fatal violence at the hands of men working in some way in the service of colonial power. Lee describes Aquash as "The voice that had grown a little too strong." Amal was the victim of a political antagonist, while Einav and Aquash died at the hands of people from their own communities, but enough symmetry exists to make the comparison valuable. By including Einav in the poem, Lee frames Amal's murder as a form of violence unlimited to cultural identity. Colonization is dangerous to everybody, women especially. Aquash's horrible death exists in this context of colonial danger, wherein the conditions of conquest reproduce themselves in the cultures of resistance, with the killing of Einav and Aquash examples of the terrible repercussions that result.

Women therefore constitute the nation by force, although they also inhabit the symbolism of national liberation. Delivered at a gathering to protest Israeli brutality in the Gaza Strip, Lee's poem deterritorializes Indigenous women from their own subjectivities, for, like their investment in justice, the nation is necessarily inter/national.

John Trudell: Geographies of Pain

The late Santee Dakota activist, actor, musician, and poet John Trudell advocated revolutionary forms of resistance all through his life. This commitment is evident throughout his large body of songs and poems. Because many of his poems are set to music, there is no clear distinction between the two genres in his oeuvre. Trudell, like Lee, offers us an opportunity to assess the performative features of Native verse. Trudell's work sought to undermine divisions between song and poetry, and so it makes no sense to impose those distinctions here. Perhaps his best song is "Rich Man's War." An intense composition with tremendous vocal energy and cutting lyrics, "Rich Man's War" comprehensively juxtaposes class disparities with state militarism.

"Rich Man's War" mentions an array of conquered or subjugated geographies: Northern Ireland, Indian country, Harlem, Central America, Palestine. He describes Central America as bleeding and then compares its wounds to Palestine and Harlem. He then juxtaposes Three Mile Island, El Salvador, the Pine Ridge Reservation, and Belfast.[4] Trudell puts those geographies in conversation with plutocratic corruption and environmental destruction. The following stanzas develop the comparison. Trudell describes the poor starving for various things—food, land, and peace—before declaring them to be starving "for real," which has at least three different connotations: "for real" could be a colloquialism emphasizing that the starving is legitimate; "for real" might suggest a desire for more authentic experiences; or "for real" could affirm the starvation as an objective reality. Trudell goes on to condemn rich man's war for attacking all of earth's life-forms and warns against its potential to destroy the future before finishing with a repeated line, "thinking of always war."

The poor of the world—the worldly dimensions of oppression are important to Trudell's symbolism—lack the material necessities of a comfortable life. This privation exists in a system, which Trudell represents through points of geographic identification that locate causation between privilege and poverty. War, in Trudell's formulation, is necessary to the concentration of wealth in elite communities. Accrual of wealth is therefore a blood rite expressed through physical and psychological attack. It becomes a normalized aesthetic in the vocabulary of modern life.

Trudell's invocation of land connects what might be considered a Marxian analysis to a specific decolonial framework; he conjoins class solidarity and liberationist politics to proffer a comprehensive vision of wordly disruption. The idea of "starving for land" is not merely a metaphor; it accurately describes a conception of land as sustenance, something tactile and knowable without which survival becomes exceedingly difficult. The difficulties of survival do not imply a sort of spiritual death but recognize the wildlife and agriculture that enabled Native peoples to flourish and produced ways of living squelched by colonization and its industrial economies. The "rich man's war" is not simply conflict in the interests of the wealthy, but a project of wealth accumulation. The reliance on war becomes habitual. The line "thinking of always war" inverts the normal indication of constancy through its modification of a noun rather than an adjective. By thinking of always war, the rich continuously pursue their own material interests. War and personhood become coterminous, one always the defining feature of the other.

Palestine enters into the poem through an inter/national structure, put into conversation with Central America, which is similarly bleeding. The rich man's war is global, a necessary factor in the era of colonization. Imperialism requires foreign resources; militarism demands victims. Their apparatus occupies vast space for research and development. In Trudell's mind, Palestine exists alongside and within multiple geographies. It is both cog and machinery. It comprises a global phenomenon, a symbol of painful reality. The places whose wounds Trudell names have little in common but their bleeding. The rich man's war requires their destruction. Three Mile Island stands out in the stanza as a different kind of place, a nuclear facility among the living but downtrodden. It connotes the pollution of war and colonization. These geographies melt into one another.

It is not accidental that Trudell conceptualizes Central America as "bleeding wounds" same as Palestine. As with his unusual formulation of an "always war," Trudell subverts typical speech conventions with the phrase "bleeding wounds." In its adjectival form, *bleeding* highlights the depth of the wounds in oppressed communities. As a verb, *bleeding* intimates their constant nature. Taken together, both versions deplore a sort of immanent violence central to the rich man's war. "Same as Palestine" speaks to both the outcome and the process of that war, especially in relation to its inter/national dynamics. A specific connection exists between El Salvador and Palestine. Although many Salvadoreans are of Palestinian origin, the connection is political. Israel's involvement in Central America on behalf of repressive juntas during a period of internecine conflict is well documented, as I illustrate in chapter 1. By highlighting the mutual suffering of Palestine and El Salvador, Trudell damns Israel without even mentioning it. A sophisticated geopolitical analysis exists in the imaginaries of allusion.

These allusions illuminate class warfare, both literal and metaphorical. Trudell connects politics to states of being, connecting the conditions of modernity to nihilism and insanity. He wonders if today's humans are even living, suggesting that if anything it is a life of lies. The stanza finishes with a bleak assessment of industrial society, accusing it of being responsible for anger and a perfunctory existence. Industrial society, according to Trudell, induces anger and ennui. Civility presupposes nihilism and insanity. Trudell describes robotic subjects entrapped by the hypnotic violence of late capitalism. This condition prevents us from exercising memory—that is to say, it erases histories and identities, sacrificing them to the anonymous movement of capital. We have no agency because our imaginations have been pre-ordained by the logic of elimination. This logic underlines the founding of the United States and is therefore indivisible from the industrial malaise that permeates its current landscape. We are born into a set of conditions that endlessly reproduce settler violence even where it is absent from discourse, language, and consciousness.

I do not read "Rich Man's War" as bleak, however. It possesses moments of foreboding, but ultimately it is an affirmation of resilience in the face of nihilistic industry. The poem and its accompanying music never lose faith in the spaces of the world damaged by the march of capitalist progress. Trudell's inclusion of Palestine in the list of oppressed geographies illuminates its metonymic importance to vocabularies of global liberation. Given its position as one of many sites of metonymy, we cannot say that Palestine embodies inter/nationalism in "Rich Man's War," but it would be fair to suggest that Palestinians deeply inform articulations of the inter/national. If the rich man perpetually thinks of "always war," then victims of that thinking always survive to narrate the memories they were not supposed to have.

Carter Revard: Questioning Imperialism

An accomplished author in numerous genres, Carter Revard offers a temperate counterpart to Trudell's breakneck energy. I juxtapose the two because Revard's poem "A Response to Terrorists" has crucial thematic similarities to "Rich Man's War," though it is stylistically different. "A Response to Terrorists" is notable for its images of spectacular violence and its topical content. The poem is conversational, deploying a second-person narrative and assuming the structure of a private chat or public lecture. Like Trudell, Revard situates Palestine within inter/national paradigms.

"A Response to Terrorists" provides a series of rhetorical questions. One of them begins with loaded histories of dispossession:

Oh sure,
it seems unlikely that the Acoma
will buy out Kerr-McGee
and claim New Mexico as theirs, or that
Cayugas, Mohawks and Oneidas
will get the Adirondacks back
and run a leveraged buyout of
the Chase Manhattan, Rupert Murdoch, and the Ivy
    League.[5]

Thus framed, Revard presents the question, which is more defiant than searching:

But if they did,
would they be citizens at last of the great
Imperial Order, rather than our kind of
small endangered cultures where the sense
of needing every one of us,
of being the tip of growth, the quick
of living earth,
is borne in on us by our smallness,
our clear fragility?

The "But if" intimates an absence of literal inquiry, yet Revard does not employ fantastical rhetoric simply to conjure a singular conclusion. *They* refers to living people still dispossessed of resources and ancestral lands. Revard implies—or at least considers the possibility—that the dispossession plays a significant role in creating modern Native cultural identities. He worries that success, as defined by imperialist standards, constitutes (or might constitute) an act of erasure. The Native, then, can never escape colonization because to overcome it is simultaneously to reproduce the conditions in which it occurred in the first place.

Revard cannot be read as renouncing decolonization, however. His critique targets the systematic dominance of capitalism and imperialism. More pointedly, he reaffirms the survival of the Native nations that exist (and sometimes thrive) within the hegemon. Chase Manhattan, Rupert Murdoch, and the Ivy League—in symbolic form, capitalism, propaganda, and plutocracy—comprise the "Imperial Order," a term notable for its properness and its allusion to the chilling implications of authoritarianism. The Imperial Order is impersonal, a place where not every person is needed, resulting in a human surplus reminiscent of the rich man's stratum in Trudell's poem. Revard juxtaposes the grandiloquent Imperial Order with the smallness and fragility of the Native, ironic descriptors that serve to validate resilience. The fragility of which Revard speaks is "clear," though it is unclear whether the adjective bespeaks clarity or conspicuousness. No matter the interpretation, it complexifies Indigenous nations (Acoma, the Haudenosaunee, and so forth), thus enacting the dynamism necessary to survival. That survival will not occur through the ordered violence of linear progress.

Readers may suspect that Revard plays with the tropes of Native nationalism, particularly in the final two lines of the second stanza, but the poem in total reveals a more sophisticated vision. "A Response to Terrorists" continues:

> It's feeling powerful and yet
> afraid that fuels killing, it's
> knowing we are weak and brave
> that lets us want to live
> and let live.

Revard is uncharacteristically frank here, avoiding symbolism and asking readers/listeners to unpack his inversion of psychological binaries instead. To put it crudely, Revard unambiguously puts forward a moral proposition. He answers it simultaneously: power and fear, in tandem, are less desirable than weakness and courage. Or, if we choose a more forceful interpretation, power coupled with fear is a recipe for imperial violence.

Revard anatomizes the mentalities of colonialism and militarism. He impugns the mythologies of late capitalism, ascribing benign peoplehood to those who value life as a basic expression of their mere existence. This dynamic emerges through sweeping historical pronouncements. To begin the poem, Revard writes:

> It seems you can't
> stay bottom dog too long

before some other
outbottoms you. Frankly,
speaking as an Indian I admit
it's easier to be noble and smile
while vanishing, just as for Martin Luther King
in prison it was easier than
for Andrew Young as Ambassador—

Revard suggests that there is a psychic benefit to disempower-
ment. To remain a geopolitical underdog allows for a certain kind
of innocence, absent from the brutal requisites of power:

and last war's victims of the Holocaust may
be next war's seekers of Lebensraum
in Lebanon or the West Bank: the Palestinians are
the ones in concentration camps, these days.
Isn't there some way we might
get out from under without finding ourselves
on top and smothering others?

This inclusion of Palestine offers terrific framing for the poem's central question. Edward Said referred to the Palestinians as "the victims of the victims" and extracted copious philosophical material
from this tragic formulation.[6] (Mahmoud Mamdani's *When Victims Become Killers* raises comparable questions.) Revard examines similar complexities. That Palestine so usefully frames Revard's
theme indicates how Native and Palestinian histories overlap. Nearly
all settler societies claim to be (or actually are) escaping some form
of persecution, lending credence to Revard's observation that lift-
ing up can occur by pushing down.

The most common term in today's imperial lexicon is *terrorist,*
the demographic Revard purports to address. (Natives are not exempt from this terminology, but the widespread condemnation of
their supposedly violent nature largely occurred before today's connotations of the word.) Revard rejects the unidirectional applica-
tion of *terrorist,* wondering if terrorism is a necessary precondition
of "finding ourselves on top." In its popular usage, terrorism points
to destructive violence that seeks to supplant the achievements of

modern democracy; in Revard's usage, terrorism is inseparable from the creation of modern democracy itself. In fact, terrorism is the operating principle of what we euphemistically call progress. It is unclear to which terrorists Revard directs his poem. We can surmise that his audience is the self-assured consumer for whom terrorism always describes the Other. Revard may be addressing world leaders, particularly those who deploy terrorism in order to fight terrorists. It is safe to say that he does not mean to impugn those, like the Palestinians, commonly dismissed as terroristic. The ambiguity of Revard's usage provides the poem a stark precision, one that forces the reader to consider himself or herself in frameworks much easier to imagine as relevant to a different breed of human.

Zionism does not escape Revard's chaotic reclassifications. One might observe that Zionism is the central idea from which taxonomical disorder emerges. Rather than situating Palestine as a symbol of global struggle for justice, as do Trudell and Lee, Revard invokes it as an exemplar of redundant histories. He raises a set of existential questions through geopolitical episodes, ascribing a type of humanity to the dispossessed by virtue of their unwillingness, or inability, to play the role of historical victor. The dangers of progress are omnipresent, though, nowhere so visibly as in the rapid transformation of Jews from concentration camp survivors to overseers.

Lee Maracle

Maracle is a vocal proponent of Palestinian liberation, an orientation that regularly informs her poetry. I focus on one poem in particular, "Song to a Palestinian Child," from her collection *Bent Box*. I choose this poem over several others—*Bent Box* alone pays homage to women from across the Southern Hemisphere—because of its complex possibilities despite a set of conspicuous commitments. Maracle manages this accomplishment in much of her poetry. In the case of "Song to a Palestinian Child," she illustrates an especially adept use of terminological and symbolic ambiguity.

The poem is short, so let us examine it in two halves. The first half:

I hear a voice calling from a place far away
The voice of a girl child very much like my own

of green grass and rich soil is Palestine.

Bombs crash about her levelling her home
Clutching an olive branch she raises a defiant fist

of deep roots and copper sun is Palestine.[7]

Maracle's primary message is obvious: she describes a Palestinian girl who resists bombardment with steadfast dignity. Maracle alludes to a deep connection, likely based on her recognition of the shared circumstances of being colonized, though age, ecology, and gender appear to be factors. She articulates empathy for the Palestinian "girl child." She does little to conceal her admiration of the character.

The ambiguity exists in Maracle's usage rather than her message. Although it might be ridiculous to speculate that the girl Maracle describes is not in Palestine, the possibility exists, however unlikely, because Maracle does not explicitly locate her in a named geography. The girl is simply "from a place far away." This formulation does not fully clarify the girl's present location, only that she is from whatever land is under discussion. Nor does it unequivocally name the "place" as Palestine. The girl could be a Native who reminds Maracle of Palestine. She could be a younger version of Maracle herself, or a blood relation, or a spiritual relation. We might consider these readings a stretch bordering on silly, but I would counter that Occam's razor does not apply to poetry. We have to consider even the most unlikely possibility, for it is in these impossibilities that a poem's most significant meaning sometimes exists. Deterritorializing Palestine would be the sort of move perfectly in keeping with Maracle's thematic commitment. If the girl is in Palestine, then Maracle's ambiguity serves to reinforce the obvious. If she is elsewhere, then Maracle has globalized Palestine as a defiant symbol. The title strongly suggests a reading of the girl child as Palestinian in ethnicity, but this reading nevertheless relies on limiting the ethnic to specific biologies.

The girl child's abstruse positionality accounts for another example of Maracle's creative ambiguity. Who is she in relation to

Maracle? (I assume Maracle to be the narrator, perhaps foolishly; the narration adds another element of ambiguity.) "The voice of a girl child very much like my own" provides no concrete modifiers. Does "the voice" or the "girl child" modify "my own"? If it is the "girl child," then Maracle suggests that she has a daughter who reminds her of the (apparent) Palestinian. If "the voice" performs the modification, then Maracle indicates that the girl child uses her voice in the same manner as the narrator. (Or vice versa in both cases.) Finally, it is possible to read the line simply as identifying a deep commonality between the narrator and the girl child.

Let us take a look at the second half of the poem as a potential site of clarity:

> I see a child rising from a place far away
> In one hand an olive branch in the other a gun
>
> of much sweat and red blood is Palestine.
>
> I hear you calling me. Raise my banner high
> (Victory), victory to Palestine I answer in kind
>
> of humble tears my salute to Palestine.

Here the sensual perspective of the poem shifts from audial to visual before returning to the audial. Now Maracle sees the child, an indication of either superhuman ability or a bond expressed through allegorical vision. (We will assume it is the latter.) This shift to sight emphasizes a slightly different sort of bond, that of an envisioned affiliation. The ability to see a place that is "far away" illustrates a rejection of the parameters of orthodox geography. We exist in proximities that do not cohere to physical contiguity. We are close in one another's vision and thus in our consciousness. Maracle employs a deeply feeling version of inter/nationalism.

This section of "Song to a Palestinian Child" clarifies some of the ambiguity of usage. The answer to the narrator's relationship with the child is not necessarily found in pronouns or modifiers but in the tactile symbols of Palestinian nationalism. The first half of the poem references an olive branch in juxtaposition with a raised fist. The second half juxtaposes the olive branch with a gun, a clear reference to Yasser Arafat's famous 1974 speech to the UN General Assembly in which he proclaimed, "Today I come bearing an olive branch in one hand, and the freedom fighter's gun in the other. Do not let the olive branch fall from my hand. I repeat, do not let the olive branch fall from my hand."[8]

Maracle also deploys imagery of "deep roots" and "copper sun," each an amalgamation of metaphor and physical symbolism. The roots can refer to, say, olive trees, some of which date to biblical times; or they can highlight the cultural depth of Indigeneity (in this case in relation to the land of Palestine). The copper sun evokes rich possibilities. It puts readers in mind of skin gilded by the sun; the implements of an ancient culture; a life-sustaining solar object at dusk or dawn; and the vividness of sunlight drenching the bodies of those determined to survive. Of particular interest is how Maracle renders these images through "of/is" formulations in the single-line stanzas—for example, "of much sweat and red blood is Palestine," an unmistakable reference to the closeness of Natives and Palestinians. In fact, the explicit identification of that closeness provides much of the poem's ambiguity. Maracle tells us that she is discussing Palestinians and Natives; she just does not tell us precisely when discussion of either occurs. "Is Palestine" could well be a reference to Native decolonization in addition to, or instead of, Palestinian symbology.

Despite these competing possibilities, we can infer certain meanings based on Maracle's structural choices. The coloring of her diction—"copper," "olive," "green"—suggests a Palestinian landscape, but one that has entered into the consciousness of the North American indigene. The child calls to the narrator, who echoes the shout of "victory," which is a political compulsion in addition to a spiritual encounter. The child and the narrator recognize the necessity of mutual liberation. Their mutual deployment of *victory* as a verbal conjunction bespeaks kinship borne of both suffering and aspiration. The two characters resist together; their resistance is a form of celebration.

Although Maracle provides no direct reference to Native characters, thus rendering the narrator's nationality unclear, we ought to remember that "Song to a Palestinian Child" is not a stand-alone poem. It exists in a collection of verse published as a book. These organizational factors provide each entry multiple contexts. In the context of Maracle's propensity throughout *Bent Box* to use a first-person narrator, it might be accurate to identify an autobiographical voice in "Song." Even if Maracle technically is not in the poem, she is certainly of it. She understands that the Palestinian requires her presence. In turn, she readily provides it, along with the sensual features of inter/national kinship. Maracle's poem is a song of many things, primarily of the importance of words to an enduring spirit. The poem sings and it represents the transmission of song. It features the women so prominent in Erica Violet Lee's narratives.

Perhaps more than any other Native poet, Maracle evokes Palestine and the Palestinians. These evocations highlight a geopolitical understanding of colonization in America and Palestine, but they also propound an amalgamation of the destinies of Natives and Palestinians, informed by the congruities of the past, as understood in the present. Only in these cyclical frameworks can Maracle harmonize the red blood of Palestine.

Edgar Gabriel Silex's Acts of Love

Silex's collection *Acts of Love* travels many different places. In addition to being geographically wide-ranging, the collection possesses diverse content. Silex crafts what might be called love and political poems traversing various linguistic, stylistic, and thematic boundaries. Of most interest here is the poem "Chief Nanay Appears in the Holy Land," devoted almost exclusively to Palestine. It begins:

> a Palestinian
> no legs one hand
> spent the last
> several months
> fleeing soldiers
> out to kill him[9]

Before moving into content, note that I say the poem is *almost* exclusively devoted to Palestine. Each stanza appears to take place in Palestine, but Silex frames "Chief Nanay" around a historical figure who, an asterisk affixed to the end of the title explains, "was a Chiricahua Apache wounded fourteen different times defending his land."

The poem goes on to describe the fleeing Palestinian having both legs and one arm "blown off," presumably by soldiers who are Israeli, though Silex does not ever name Israel. It would take an extraordinary leap of logic to suggest that the people Silex paints as oppressors are other than Israeli, though his choice not to identify them by nationality or ethnicity provides critical opportunities. My reading is that he refuses to name them because they are unworthy of respect or are incidental to the narrative and because he contextualizes their behavior as universal to settler colonization. Severely compromised physically, the protagonist nevertheless remains defiant:

in the end he used
his only hand
to shoot at soldiers
advancing
on his house

he couldn't move
so he stayed

The phrase "on his house" recurs from the preceding stanza, in which the protagonist loses his legs to advancing soldiers. This house does not simply locate action, but serves a metaphorical role as a rooted structure on ancestral land. The soldier attacks the Palestinian not where he resides, but where he lives. The soldiers are "advancing" in both stanzas because they arrive from elsewhere — they are foreigners, essentially, a pointed description of those who inhabit a settler army.

The imagery Silex uses almost reads like caricature, but it manages to simultaneously impart powerful commentary. We do not know if the protagonist dies, though he clearly is severely injured, even if only symbolically. He resists, however, with all that is left of his body, propelled by the clarity of his mind. He cannot be incapacitated or eliminated because his inhabitance constitutes place.

Leaving is not an option because place defines his inhabitance. Because the soldiers shoot his legs, he remains even more firmly planted on the land. Colonial violence motivates increased articulations of Indigeneity. It also motivates Indigenous violence. The protagonist of "Chief Nanay," like Nanay himself, is neither passive nor conflicted. He shoots back.

This process has occurred over the span of "several months," which raises interesting temporal and rhetorical questions. How can the protagonist flee if "he couldn't move"? Three main possibilities exist: (1) in Silex's imagination, flight transforms into permanence, a kind of symbolic transit; (2) the Palestinian has fled home after being in the field; (3) it is actually the soldiers in flight. The first two possibilities might be interchangeable, while the third is an interpretive outlier. Silex's grammar allows for the chance that soldiers are fleeing. Let us reread the relevant stanza: "a Palestinian / no legs one hand / spent the last / several months / fleeing soldiers / out to get him." If "fleeing soldiers" modifies "a Palestinian," then the protagonist is in flight. However, if we read it as an independent clause, then the soldiers are fleeing.

Consider: Silex does not use commas or periods, nor do his lines begin with proper nouns. (The only word capitalized in the body of the poem is "Palestinian.") Nothing stops us, then, from reading "fleeing soldiers / out to get him" as a stand-alone sentence. If the soldier, not the protagonist, is fleeing, then the poem emphasizes the rootedness of Palestinians to their ancestral land. If it is the protagonist, we can render the same reading, but with the caveat that the soldiers' presence is not permanent. Similarly, when the protagonist "couldn't move," how is "couldn't" deployed? Does it indicate a physical or mental/emotional motivation? If the former, then the protagonist is afflicted by a temporal problem; if the latter, then he or she refuses a destiny invented by the colonizer. Given the tenor of the poem, which highlights the immanence of resistance, the latter interpretation seems more viable.

Despite no mention of Natives or the United States in the poem's body, a persistent sense of America nevertheless pervades the narrative. The title and small biographical note about Chief Nanay provide the pervasion. The effect is a strange geographic (and political) amorphousness: the reader can easily confuse the location of the action between America and Palestine. This effect is compounded by Silex's amalgamation of mythical and realistic imagery. "Chief Nanay" is not what might be called a historical poem, but it encompasses vast histories. Nanay's appearance in the Holy Land expands the geography of Indian country into mythological settler narratives of Indians-as-lost-tribes and America as a land of milk and honey.

He also expands that geography into a specific political climate; for it is not merely the "Holy Land" into which Chief Nanay enters, but modern Palestine, a nation occupied by a foreign state and beset by the violence of that occupation. Is Chief Nanay the Palestinian protagonist? It is likely. It is also possible that Nanay is a metaphor of the Palestinian. We can say with certainty that Nanay, a person with tremendous capacity for resistance, comes to inhabit the land of Palestine. The verb *appears* in the poem's title suggests that Nanay's time in Palestine is temporary, but that would mean Palestinian resistance is temporary, as well, because Nanay inhabits a form of timelessness contingent on the native's refusal of submission.

Chief Nanay is thus alive. He appears in Palestine because he recognizes Israel's style of colonization and the importance, or the imminence, of struggle against it. Nanay's travels, whether spiritual or metaphorical (or possibly even physical), highlight shared histories of displacement and resilience. The relaxed grammar of the poem further illuminates a blurring of spatial and temporal convention. The reader gets the sense that Chief Nanay has visited lots of places. It is no coincidence that Silex chose to document his visit to Palestine.

Darwish and Means

Now we arrive at analysis of poetry in tandem. Native and Palestinian poets regularly converse with one another, and it would not be too difficult to write a significant piece about those conversations, both direct and oblique. Yet Mahmoud Darwish and Russell Means interact explicitly—or, to be more accurate, Means interacts with Darwish. This speech is reactive and prescient.

In the spirit of Darwish and Means's interchange, I assess their poems in tandem rather than sectioning them against one another. Darwish was a critic and politician in addition to a writer, but he achieved his greatest recognition as a poet. Means, on the other hand, is not generally described as a writer—though his memoir *Where White Men Fear to Tread* is well known—having derived his fame from activism, acting, and politics. We can therefore say that an important distinction between Darwish and Means exists not only in ethnicity, language, and geography, but also in terms of profession, with Darwish having had the advantage of life as a full-time poet.

"The 'Red Indian's' Penultimate Speech to the White Man" is one of Darwish's most famous offerings.[10] Written in an epic style, the poem has seven chapters and alternates between narrative and verse. It opens with one of many proverbial observations:

> Then, we are who we are in the Mississippi. We have what is left to us of
>
> > yesterday.[11]

Darwish locates the "Red Indian" in the Mississippi (River? Basin? State? Valley?), conjuring a frontier (or freewheeling) image of the United States. (The term "Red Indian," which surely sounds archaic, or worse, to the American ear, is a literal translation from Arabic: *Hindi Ahmar,* the appellation for North and South American Indigenous peoples.) "What is left to us" intimates a controlling power; "Then" intimates prior stories or a focused axis of identification. Darwish thus visualizes the Native as an embodiment of manifold histories. He or she narrates the poem because Darwish's recognition of Native autonomy necessitates his concession.

In his counterpoem, "The Song of the Palestinian," Means recognizes Darwish's theme of manifold history:

> Euro-male, where do you come from?
> Is not your mother sacred?
> Is not your mother's life sacred?
> Is not her children sacred?
> Do you understand rebirth?[12]

Means takes it as a given that Darwish positions his Native narrator as speaking to "Euro-males," though Darwish's narrator never actually names an audience. It is a safe assumption based on the poem's content and represents a tactic evident throughout Means's offering: a recapitulation of Darwish's themes in terser language. For example, Darwish writes, "Were you not born of women? Did you not suckle as we did / the milk of longing for mothers?" Means critiques the same colonial society implicated by Darwish's narrator. In turn, he positions the Palestinian as the inheritor of colonial histories. Darwish positions the Native as their original victim.

Of interest is both poems' emphasis on the colonizer's lapsed humanity (or perhaps his instinct). Darwish's Native narrator wonders:

> You have what you desire: the new Rome, the Sparta of
>   technology
>   and the ideology
>   of madness,
> but as for us, we will escape from an age we haven't yet
>   prepared our
>   anxieties for.

Means's Palestinian narrator asks a series of questions that I read as literal rather than rhetorical:

> Do you understand being free?
> Do you understand the sand?
> Do you understand the rivers?
> Do you understand the olive tree?
> Do you understand the rocks?
> Do you understand the air you breathe
> Do you understand peace of mind?

Everything about colonization, in this formulation, is *unnatural*. Neither author deploys that term, but it underlies the concept of an escape from the ideologies of technological madness. Neither Darwish nor Means seeks a nostalgic return to precolonial polities, but both rely on the past to contextualize the conditions of Indigenous survival. Darwish, for example, writes: "A long time will pass for our present to become a past like us. / But first, we will march to our doom, we will defend the trees we wear / and defend the bell of the night, and a moon we desire over our huts."

These images foreground Means's repetitious use of *understand,* a term of myriad value that in "The Song of the Palestinian" references nature and the peace of mind available from an unspoiled environment. Both poets get at notions of balance and consistency as against the destructiveness of forced marches into "doom," which might stand in for modernity, capitalism, or industrialized economies. Their styles and language differ considerably, and their thematic concerns differ at least slightly, but they work with the same body of philosophical material. This material explores the tensions between Indigenous sociopolitical systems and the vicissitudes of top-down democracy. The present is in constant dialogue with the past, not just as a matter of recouping cultural memory, but also as a technique of physical survival. The past allows the indigene the ability to know what it is like "being free."

It is easy to forget which body of text is meant to represent the Native vis-à-vis the Palestinian, a particular benefit of reading the poems in tandem. With the Palestinian poet writing from the point of view of the "Red Indian" and the Native poet writing from the point of view of the Palestinian, the reader can easily invert ethnic subjectivities, which appears to be one of Means's main goals in responding to Darwish. The potential inversion of ethnic subjectivities illuminates the utility of the poet as cultural shapeshifter. By mimicking Darwish's approach, Means completes a process beyond Darwish's purview: exploration of the discontinuities of Native histories as they have extended into Palestine. One can read that theme in "The 'Red Indian's' Penultimate Speech to the White Man," but only obliquely, and only by evoking an imagined subjectivity based on knowledge of Darwish's ethnic/national background.

The recouping of cultural memory, Darwish's narrator implies, requires the presence of a cosmos and a landscape, no matter how distant or degraded:

Come, let's split the light in the force of shadow, take what
    you want

of the night, and leave two stars for us to bury our dead in
  their orbit,
take what you want of the sea, and leave two waves for us
  to fish in,
take the gold of the earth and the sun, and leave the land of
  our names
and go back, stranger, to your kin . . . and look for India.

Means's narrator speaks with more urgency, deploying notions of
predestination (or perhaps of the inevitability of material redress):
"There is rebirth. / I will return as lightning." A notable similarity
can be found in both poems' use of naturalist imagery. They recognize a force of human organization absent from the ideologies
of colonization.

This section of "The 'Red Indian's' Penultimate Speech to the
White Man" shows Darwish at his least abstruse. The reader can
sense defiance in the tone of the final line, and an uncharacteristic
moment of inhospitability in calling the white man a stranger. (I say
"uncharacteristic" because much of the poem seeks an unspecified
coexistence with the settler.) "Stranger" certainly can be a neutral or
even friendly greeting, but in relation to the rest of the narrative I
view it as an accusation. The caustic ending of the line ". . . and
look for India" intimates frustration and exhaustion (and possibly ridicule). A generous reading might call it helpful advice. It is
this portion of the poem that Means seizes when he declares that
Palestinian retribution is inevitable and will be swift and decisive,
like lightning.

Of greater interest is the discourse leading to the eye-opening
line about India. The Native offers the settler a compromise born
of desperation: satisfy your avarice but leave something behind that
we might survive. The Native understands that colonization exists
in totality. It occupies even the sea and the stars. This reality explains
why Darwish's narrator often reflects on the past as a form of frac-
tured survival. The appeal to existing in peace with the leftovers
of conquest is reminiscent of Carter Revard's reflections on the
price of modernity in "A Response to Terrorists." We see this sort
of reflection across Native poetry that explores the worldly fallout

of conquest. It identifies tensions between the demands of postindustrial economic success and what Ojibwe writer Gerald Vizenor calls "survivance," a portmanteau of "survival" and "resistance." In some cases, the poets hypothesize something more intense than tension, an irreconcilability of tradition and industry. This irreconcilability is not fixed, but presented to the reader for consideration. It represents a moral, economic, or philosophical question that cannot occur without the deeply restricted modes of (political and ecological) autonomy that result from ongoing colonization.

Means's narrator attributes the problem to majoritarian obliviousness. He declares in response to the series of ostensible questions I quoted earlier, "I think not." The verb *think* positions the narrator as a cogitative being in contrast to the ignorant colonizer. The line is both flippant and emphatic. If the Zionist does not, or cannot, understand freedom, sand, rivers, olive trees, rocks, the atmosphere, or peace of mind, the Zionist does not, or cannot, understand Palestine. "The Song of the Palestinian" therefore creates an allegory of the unthinking colonizer as against the portions of humanity capable of responsibly inhabiting the earth. The narrator's answer to the colonizer's inability to sustain life on Indigenous geographies is for the native to return, swiftly and unapologetically. It is a poetic version of a specific Indigenist philosophy of uncompromised resistance.

Darwish's narrator is more cautious (or skeptical, perhaps). Yet, beyond the exhausted offers of coexistence, the narrator too implicates the colonizer's ignorance:

> You will lack, white ones, the memory of departure from the
> Mediterranean
> you will lack eternity's solitude in a forest that doesn't
> overlook the
> chasm
> you will lack the wisdom of fractures, the setback of war
> you will lack a rock that doesn't obey the rapid flow of
> time's river
> you will lack an hour of meditation in anything that might
> ripen in you

a necessary sky for the soil, you will lack an hour of hesitation
    between
                         one path
and another, you will lack Euripides one day, the Canaanite
    and the
                         Babylonian poems

Darwish, albeit speaking through the voice of a Native, attaches the speech to the Middle East through reflections on the Mediterranean, Canaan, and Babylon. The American colonizer draws on such taproots for his national identity, but he will be unable to maintain these connections. The prediction (or threat) that the "white ones" will "lack Euripides one day" is performed through the poem's structure, which reproduces that of *Medea,* whose titular character returned from exile to conquer her homeland of Colchis. (There are dozens of interpretive possibilities in Darwish's invocation of Euripides, as well as his invocation of Canaan and Babylon.) By returning to the landscapes of his childhood, Darwish positions the Native as an effective narrator of Palestinian dispossession. He thus binds the Native to a foreign history that the Native has been forced to assume. Underlying the connection between Darwish's Native and Darwish himself is the impoverishment of conquest.

Means distills much of "The 'Red Indian's' Penultimate Speech to the White Man" to blunt condemnation, but his distillation well captures the essence of Darwish's poem. By speaking in the voice of a Palestinian obliged to confront the conquest of America, Means binds the Palestinian to the aspirations of the Native. He vocalizes the project that for Darwish is merely implicit.

Conclusion: Poetic Transgression

The imagery of Palestine and Palestinians in Native poetry supersedes instrumentalism. As a thematic device, it performs important features of inter/nationalism, including the juxtaposition of Natives and Palestinians as mutual actors in a wide-ranging struggle to reorganize the world. I acknowledge that my reading of this thematic device, as well as broader poetic phenomena, is constrained by both logistics and imagination. This acknowledgment is not a plea to avoid criticizing my analysis, but an invitation to join in conversation around this topic and its attendant possibilities.

The presence of Palestine in Native poetry is limited to work published within the past few decades. Indeed, the poetic impetus to invoke colonized communities around the world is generally (but not strictly) a recent development, though Native poets have always exhibited pan-Indian commitments (I use a quaint term here, but one that reasonably describes the practice within its own milieu). These elements of inter/nationalism are modern, though they seek to undermine the commonplaces of modernity.

We encounter serious problems of time and structure by accepting a fixed notion of "Native poetry." The cartographies of Native expression, oral and written, do not, and should not be made to, cohere with the taxonomical norms of U.S. literary history. For this reason, my sketch of inter/nationalism in Native poetry is inherently circumscribed, in precisely the same way that any reckoning with this impossibly complex category illuminates the limits of criticism. Yet, impossible complexity is one of the benefits of inter/nationalist methodologies, which aim to accentuate the vastness of dialogic possibility rather than reducing it to the vocabularies of neoliberal pragmatism.

A few things about the uses of Palestine in Native poetry emerge from the samples I have examined. Native writers who mention or explore Palestine often do so as a mode of self-reflection, which indicates that a consciousness of multiplicity informs Native art. The artists reinvent notions of Indigenous self and society in part through cultural and political colloquy. Cultural and political colloquy emerges from a liberationist desire and national survival. America and Palestine coincide. If the lifeblood of poetry is symbolism, then Palestine offers wonderful symbolic possibilities for the Native poet.

5.
WHY AMERICAN INDIAN STUDIES SHOULD BE IMPORTANT TO PALESTINE SOLIDARITY

■   ■   ■

I began this book with an assessment of Palestine's role in American Indian studies in which I argue that Palestine is now a legible theme in the field. I am less confident about the stability of American Indian studies in Palestine solidarity communities, particularly the academic groupings in which Palestine exists as a site of inquiry. (I do not use the more trenchant "Palestine studies" because I locate this site of inquiry in multiple fields: ethnic studies, American Indian studies, Indigenous studies, American studies, literary criticism, sociology, anthropology, history, Asian American studies, critical race theory, and Middle East studies. Palestine studies is fundamentally an interdisciplinary concern.) This chapter articulates a rationale for why American Indian studies is useful to the study of Palestine. The main factor of this rationale suggests that American Indian studies is indispensable to the basic imperatives of Palestine solidarity.

In particular, I examine recent debates about academic freedom, faculty governance, donor influence, and the suppression of radical points of view in the context of the colonial logic by which universities are animated. I synthesize recent controversies on campus around pro-Palestine sentiment and then situate them in broader questions of educational decolonization. I further explore what it means to conduct radical work within fundamentally restrictive institutions; how the university embodies specific geographies of conquest; why Palestine solidarity work on campus must necessarily engage American Indian communities; and where sites of intellectual and political interaction might produce useful tension. A survey of recent scholarship around Indigenous nationalism—a term meant to identify struggles for self-determination, liberation, sovereignty, or decolonization—illustrates that in many ways Palestine is theorized in the absence of its strongest advocates. This is not to say that Indigenous theorists ignore Palestine. To the contrary, I suggest that advocates of Palestine limit their material and theoretical range by too frequently ignoring the work of American Indian and Indigenous studies.

A few more qualifications: I am not shy to confess that I experience difficulty in attempting to encapsulate certain ideas within the constraints and ambiguities of terminology. This problem is especially dogged in relation to the catchall of "Palestine solidarity," which accommodates scholarship, activism, law, media, and international relations. The rough usage I deploy identifies or tries to coalesce activity in the service of Palestinian liberation (cultural and geographic). How does solidarity work in an academic setting? To answer this question, we must first contemplate the parameters of an academic setting. To limit it to teaching and research, or to the peculiar topographies of campus, as most would, tacitly reinforces firm distinctions between public and private intellectual spaces. An academic setting can be found in any site of critical engagement or project of transformation. Yes, this is an impetuous definition. It is also a definition that demands recognition of work that informs or sustains material and decolonial politics. That possibility is crucial to scholarly practices seeking to extend (or undermine) the limitations of the disinterested professoriat maintained by self-appointed guardians of objectivity.

Returning to solidarity, I am not interested in the term beyond its ability to organize some type of meaning to processes of Palestinian decolonization. In other words, as regards the phrase "Palestine solidarity," the adjective is much more important than the noun, which serves to inversely modify what precedes it. "Solidarity" anchors various academic pursuits around the specter of Palestine, though the pursuits are not limited to it. In an academic setting, then, Palestine solidarity describes work in some way committed to Palestinian liberation, which necessarily encompasses inter/national geographies. That commitment need not include speechifying or protest (though it certainly can). It can entail measured commentary or theoretical intervention; pedagogical reflection or classroom praxis; epistemological analysis or close reading. If Palestine exists on campus as both subject and object, then it is crucial to map its desires and imperatives. I view solidarity as an elemental feature of Palestine studies, in much the same way that decolonial praxis influences American Indian and Indigenous studies.

Extant scholarly traditions animate this conception of Palestine. In *A Shadow over Palestine: The Imperial Life of Race in America*, Keith Feldman assesses a rich history of Palestinian theorization deeply concerned with the material realities of dispossession and the potential conditions of liberation. He writes:

> Scholars of Arab descent committed to Palestinian national liberation theorized the emergence, contours, and effects of racism in shaping the social terrain in Israel and the Occupied Palestinian Territories. Organizations like the Palestine Research Center, the Institute for Palestine Studies, and the Association of Arab American University Graduates produced a historically nuanced critique of Zionism as an extension of settler colonialism, one predicated on sharp racial distinctions not only between Arabs and Jews but also between northern European Jews and their trans-Mediterranean, Arab Jewish, and Black counterparts.[1]

Feldman illustrates that a body of critique arose from Palestinian society (in both the homeland and the diaspora) that foregrounded the later versions of anti-Zionist work that now carve an increasingly significant niche in academic spaces. Although Feldman discusses a post-1967 epoch, we might legitimately extend the tradition to the era of British Mandate rule in Palestine—for example, by citing George Antonius's landmark *The Arab Awakening*.

There is a long tradition among Palestine scholars, artists, and politicians of naming the colonization of North America as both a precursor and a complement to Zionist settlement. Dating to the 1960s, Walid Khalidi and Fayez Sayegh both situated Palestine in prior and concomitant sites of settler colonialism, including North America.[2] Their work had a profound influence on the ethos of anti-Zionism, which in many of its historical and contemporaneous manifestations is fundamentally global, in both sites of practice and articulation. More recently, Nadera Shalhoub-Kevorkian and Magid Shihade have produced copious work assessing the inter/national dynamics at play among ground-level advocates of Palestinian liberation.[3] Each scholar, along with a broader community of thinkers and theorists, treats Palestine as an embodiment of a set of worldly ideas in addition to thinking about its issues as a discrete sociopolitical and economic space. No contradiction exists between these two approaches. Rather, they illuminate the ability of creative thinkers to disaggregate particularities.

I conflate Palestine studies and Palestine solidarity because scholars and activists have already enacted this type of conflation throughout the era of Zionist colonization. I merely endeavor to render something extant into something explicit. I propose that Palestine solidarity in the United States cannot rightly limit itself to analysis of Zionism and Palestinian liberation. To be clear, it has never limited itself solely to these concerns, but neither has it fully grappled with the consequences of doing Palestine solidarity work on the lands of other dispossessed peoples. It is critical for those working on issues of justice in America to avail ourselves of Native scholars and organizers in whose ancestral lands we operate. Through their work, we can contribute to decolonial projects in the spaces we inhabit while simultaneously reinvigorating our commitment to global sites of injustice.

American Indian Studies and Academic Unfreedom

On August 2, 2014, I was two weeks from beginning a position as associate professor in American Indian studies at the University of Illinois at Urbana-Champaign (UIUC) when I was summarily terminated for delivering tweets critical of Israeli policy and Zionist ideologies. (This is merely the headline version of events. The factors underlying the termination are more complex than a wayward Twitter feed.) The university's decision resulted in a storm of remonstration from a cross section of scholars and free-speech advocates who viewed it as a violation of the First Amendment and academic hiring protocol. As of this writing, much work has been produced about the matter, but the majority of it elides the location of my hiring and firing. I have little desire to proffer a self-defense or rehearse long-standing debates about extramural speech and academic freedom. Rather, I suggest that the story of my firing illuminates useful features of the vexing relationship between American Indian studies and the corporate academy, especially as those vexed relations can be enacted through the specter of Palestine.

The location of my hiring and firing in American Indian studies is a crucial aspect of this story, perhaps its most important one. We have to consider what it means to the field that it could so flippantly become a target of managerial acrimony (in general, but also in relation to specific circumstances at UIUC). Similarly, we have to consider the discourses justifying UIUC's decision because their assumptions reproduce age-old narratives of the need for oversight of Native communities. If the forthcoming analysis can be reduced to a single observation, it would be this: the precariousness of American Indian and Indigenous studies in institutions motived by a pervasive and unnamed colonial logic has been illuminated by the conditions informing American Indian studies (AIS) at UIUC and by a particular reaction to UIUC's decision that devalues AIS as a field and Native peoples as sovereign agents.

The conditions that envelop American Indian studies at UIUC are explainable largely by racism and colonial orthodoxy. The university's erstwhile mascot, Chief Illiniwek, embodies, or broadcasts, much of the racism. Formally "retired" in 2007 by the National Collegiate Athletic Association (NCAA), the presiding body of college athletics, the chief remains an integral part of campus, community, and state culture. Before his retirement, various movements sought to outlaw the chief; after he was retired, those movements have continued in response to the chief's omnipresence on campus and throughout Champaign-Urbana. A significant number of UIUC alumni opposed the retirement; many of them sent messages of protest or threatened to withhold donations. As a result, folks affiliated with the American Indian Studies Program are often scapegoated or subject to racist discourse, some of it invective. The chief's presence thus creates an environment of constant harassment for UIUC's Indigenous residents.

The chief is more than the emblem of a culture war, though that is how he is most frequently understood. Natives and their supporters tend to view the mascot in more allegorical fashion. For instance, a 2007 statement by the American Indian Studies Program supporting the chief's retirement emphasizes, in a context of "knowledge and understanding of the histories of American Indian peoples and their cultures," the importance of an "ability to critique and set aside images that confine the perception of an entire people to a limited and narrow existence. Stereotypical images, negative or positive, are barriers to understanding, and they miseducate the public about Native Americans."[4] For the chief's supporters, the mascot symbolizes a landed tradition of state culture, but for Natives, he represents continued social, economic, and political injustice. Nearly every analysis of the chief, favorable or not, examines his effect on Natives, but in reality the chief exemplifies majoritarian angst. He is a visual symbol of the settler's attempt at belonging in America.

UIUC's administration at best tolerates the chief's continued presence, and at worst encourages it. He is the omnipresent but often unacknowledged protagonist in management's decision to strip American Indian studies of its hiring autonomy. Even the American Association of University Professors (AAUP), which investigated UIUC for violations of academic freedom (and determined the institution to be guilty), found the chief's role in my firing to be relevant: "In interviews with this subcommittee, the issue of the Chief came up repeatedly in the context of the AIS program's advocacy for the mascot's retirement, which made AIS a target of hostility for those who insisted on perpetuating the tradition."[5] The chief, we must remember, enacts and symbolizes this hostility, but he is the result of much larger problems of ongoing colonization.

The chief might also be an unwitting emblem of the discourses rationalizing UIUC's behavior, which initiated a farrago of troublesome assumptions about the viability of American Indian studies and the sustainability of Native communities. Numerous faculty around the country suggested that the hiring process was flawed or corrupt; that I lack the requisite qualifications to teach in American Indian studies; or that my scholarship is of an inferior standard (ergo, the American Indian Studies Program should not have selected me for the position). I have been defensive about all three propositions since I first heard them, but here I resist the temptation to correct the record because greater matters are at stake. I will simply point out that no evidence has yet been presented to indicate corruption or substandard scholarship.

The greater matters I reference exist in the tacit authoritarianism of these narratives. By impugning the competence of the search committee and the ethics of the department more broadly, supporters of UIUC's management rendered American Indian studies knowable according to the erstwhile induction of neoliberal common sense. American Indian studies can be knowable via the regressive strictures of doctrinal mythology, which, among other things, posit an objective analyst as the ideal scholar. Typical valuations of scholarship rely on doctrinal mythology and therefore discount forms of engagement and theorization that inform American Indian and Indigenous studies (along with a host of other fields, particularly those clustered in ethnic studies). That the faculty in American Indian studies at UIUC are inherently unqualified to evaluate their own departmental growth underscores the dangers of these smug and uncreative conceptions of intellectual labor.

Department faculty member Vicente Diaz states the issue forthrightly in his assessment of American Indian studies critic Cary Nelson, who has offered a barrage of statements reproducing the disenfranchisement of the field since my termination:

> Nelson has no qualifications in this case; he has no research or teaching or published record in comparative native studies, of indigenous cultural and historical studies. I know of no colleague or scholar in my field who cites his work for how it helps

us better understand the complex and fraught histories, struggles, perspectives, expressions of indigenousness as a category of existence and category for analyses, or as a category for analyzing the fraught line between power, politics and academic inquiry.[6]

Diaz spares diplomacy in his analysis, which is less a condemnation of a colonial prison guard than a defense of the very survival of his vocation. If we extend the logic of tacit authoritarianism vis-à-vis Native departmental sovereignty, then in essence its purveyors desire the eradication of American Indian and Indigenous studies, even if they are too refined to make that desire explicit.

We also must consider the physical realities of UIUC. Like other land-grant universities, the place itself is an artifact of colonization. To conceptualize UIUC as a rarefied institution exempt from the travails of its own history is to imply that its colonial origin has died and been replaced by something more benign. The continued ubiquity of the chief and management's opprobrium toward American Indian studies render that implication excessively optimistic. The university is a monument of history dispensed through the stateliness of permanent structures. Campus exists as a magisterial architecture of an unresolved past and a contested future. In this environment, Indigenous peoples inhabit a sort of dual mascotry: one in the service of colonial self-affirmation (the chief) and the other as the raw material of diversity pamphleteering (which itself is a form of colonial self-affirmation, though a less self-aware version). UIUC is fully reliant on the existence of Natives, but only if those Natives can be simulated through the poses of colonial playacting.

Through my hiring and termination we have a distinct material example of American Indian studies and Palestine as a joint endeavor. My hiring illuminates a move toward inter/national praxis, while my firing underlines the precariousness that attends American Indian and Indigenous studies in U.S. academe. (The American Indian Studies Program was in the process of transitioning to Indigenous studies, in part to accommodate work on the Pacific.) The study of Indigenous peoples has always entailed specific challenges, from methodological debates to institutional marginalization, but in an era of restricted budgets (excluding management) and increased corporate dominion, pressure points intensify. Their intensification arises from a preponderance of neoliberal conventions extending off campus to phenomena such as legislative hostility to higher education, plutocratic governance, and economic disenfranchisement, which affect protocol all the way to the level of academic departments. Campuses both arbitrate and internalize socioeconomic iniquity.

With this context in mind, we are forced to consider an obvious question: is Palestine the tipping point of American Indian studies in the neoliberal imagination? That is to say, does the presence of Palestine in American Indian studies summon additional burdens that imperil the future of the field (to say nothing of its present)? The question may be obvious, but the answer is far from self-evident. Instinct might suggest that in the case of UIUC, Palestine helped actualize a heretofore mediated form of oppression. A quick reading of the situation suggests that the considerable force of Zionist pressure combined with extant forms of susceptibility, derived mainly from colonial racism, finally dissolved a tenuous association between corporation (UIUC) and collective (American Indian Studies Program) based on the inherent weakness of toleration and diversity as relational principles.

Yet it is worth considering whether American Indian studies in fact exerts a different type of pressure on Zionists, one to which they are not fully accustomed. If we put Natives at the center of the imbroglio, then it opens interesting possibilities for the exploration of Zionism's fragile id when it comes to violent projects of self-fulfillment. Many Zionists can accept recognition of the vicious process of state building in America because they do not implicate themselves in it and because U.S. colonization widely (though inaccurately) is seen to be completed. Regarding Israeli colonization, on the other hand, there is no equivalent sense of moral or historical distance. (I accept that these observations generalize, but would argue that they accurately describe a visible discursive phenomenon that, while nuanced and localized, produces consistent philosophical outcomes.) The convergence of American Indian studies and

Palestine implicates the Zionist in two sites of colonization. A certain anxiety attends the recognition given that plenty of Zionists are unwilling to acknowledge even the existence of Israeli colonization.

The question of Jewish whiteness also bears on this anxiety. To argue whether American Jews are properly white misses the point. Neither whiteness nor Jewishness is a stable category, so we can recognize unresolved, amorphous tension around the question of race and American Jews. There have undoubtedly been political and rhetorical moves to inscribe American Jews as normatively white, however. By relentlessly aligning itself with the grandeur of American values, Zionism makes a bold statement of assimilation into a settler majority. A quandary emerges: if American Jews are white, then they accept complicity in U.S. colonization; if they are to evade that complicity, then they must disavow themselves of white normativity, which deifies the mythos of American conquest. Any narrative that juxtaposes U.S. and Israeli colonization, then, undermines the tidy, insular logic of Zionist redemption.

U.S. colonization is not limited to whiteness, though, even if the vagaries of whiteness as a civic taxonomy inform its disposition. In turn, the anti-Zionism inherent to Palestine solidarity is an especially rich source of analysis. (I argue below that those involved in Palestine solidarity should not divest themselves of responsibility for U.S. colonization.) In the framework of UIUC, examining the university's decision in light of department and field rather than individual shows how inter/national kinship disrupts the corporate machinations of campus governance. Management responded with a heavy hand in my case because there was no refined strategy of informal recrimination to summon (or assert itself). Campus governing conventions rely on equilibrium between repressiveness and the participation of the repressed in their own repression. American Indian studies has to alter its very mission if it is to play the role that most university leaders desire of it, usually to enrich some version of a diversity portfolio. Challenging Zionism is not conducive to this desire.

Much of the value of American Indian and Indigenous studies exists off campus, which complicates our ability to fathom these tensions. I speak not of the research that professors conduct in faraway places, but the location of the fields' imperatives in national communities. The project of American Indian studies at UIUC, therefore, required a sort of global engagement that already contravened its ideal positionality in the eyes of management. Extending focus to Palestine enabled decolonial commitments fundamentally restricted in other departments for reasons of both methodological conservativism and lack of imagination.

My hire invited pro-Israel agitators to defend a commitment to ideological supremacy in a space generally beyond their realm of remonstration. As the connections between Native and Palestinian decolonial organizing continue to increase, however, it is likely that Zionist pressure will become a regular feature of American Indian and Indigenous studies (as it already is in numerous fields). This pressure will not merely seek to curtail criticism of Israel, but will actively bolster state and administrative power. After all, one of Israel's main geopolitical duties is to act as a guarantor of U.S. colonial interests. Palestine solidarity activists and scholars must respond with interventions of their own, not in order to muddle American Indian and Indigenous studies but to perform the recognition that our obligations toward the dispossessed are not limited to Palestine. They first and foremost encompass the American ground on which we stand.

Academic freedom is mostly ephemera. We should take it as a given that Natives and Palestinians have restricted access to its protections, as does anybody inhabiting bodies or spaces that in the normative imagination so readily become deviant. Restrictions on academic freedom can produce various forms of punishment, but the maintenance of academic freedom is not our primary goal. If it were, our academic freedom would not be systematically restricted in the first place. Emphasis on the injustices to which committed scholars react is a more useful place to invest our energy. The goal is to make academic freedom obsolete.

On Issues That Are Not Ours

A refrain I sometimes hear from those in American Indian or Indigenous studies is that Palestine is a worthy issue but extraneous to their concerns. I have no idea how many people believe this refrain to be true or adhere to the insularity it produces. Nobody, as far as I know, has conducted a survey of strategic preferences or assessed attitudes among Native academics vis-à-vis Israel–Palestine. My observation is anecdotal, drawn from memories of roundtables, conference panels, chitchat, and informal alliances. Sometimes a conversation will address what to do or say about Israeli war crimes, if anything at all.

I do not endeavor to convince my colleagues in American Indian and Indigenous studies that they are obligated to condemn Israel's behavior. I am disinclined to suggest any sort of obligation at all. I see the issue, despite its disaggregation and diffuseness, as an analytic possibility. On-the-ground organizing and contemporary theorization in Indian country (and elsewhere) point to increased efforts at inter/national camaraderie. As I will illustrate in the following section, recent scholarship is effectively addressing developments in Indigenous politics, scholarship, and activism. I am most interested in the potential of Palestine solidarity to make itself useful to American Indian studies and to contribute in meaningful ways to those political, scholarly, and activist developments.

The idea of non-Natives as a homogeneous mass of settlers is apocryphal and unproductive. The obvious exception is the population descended from the transatlantic slave trade, part of a constellation of groups Jodi Byrd usefully deems "arrivants," a category that provides shading to the settler/native paradigm. It can appear silly to allot various communities into different categories; it in fact is silly if the point is to merely reaffirm the categories, which amounts to an intellectual parlor game. A more worthwhile goal is to explore the ethnic cartographies of America for the purpose of addressing complexities that inform the viability of decolonization. "Settler" is a term with great moral persuasion, one that summons notions of violence in the service of citizenship. It is not a term, however, that easily lends itself to uncluttered discernment, even if it effectively describes a political and economic demographic.

What, for instance, of wartime refugees, such as Somalis, Hmong, and Iraqis? Inca-speaking migrant laborers from Central America?

I am less interested in where these groups fit within a settler-native spectrum and more interested in how their complicated experiences might allow them to more helpfully engage Native struggles for justice. They have more impetus to be attuned to continued Native dispossession than, say, the white landowners on an Indian reservation or immigrants who operate liquor stores just on the other side of the county line. I do not wish to imply that war refugees or their descendants necessarily have good politics, or that settlers necessarily do not. Rather, I suggest that differing positionalities offer different opportunities at effective solidarity. Mapping the social dynamics of the U.S. polity allows us to emphasize settler colonization as a primordial site of contestation, one whose patterns influence nearly every manner of economic, gendered, and racial interaction.

As a quick aside, the same complexities attend to the Jewish Israeli population. It is easy to apply a crude label of "settler" to a native of Brooklyn in a West Bank colony. It is less easy to be so crude in relation to other demographics (though this does not preclude the accuracy of the noun *settler*): those of Iraqi background who were coerced through Israeli violence into emigration; the Yemenis who were airlifted to Israel and suffered terribly once they landed; Ethiopian Jews who experience strident racism and whose women have faced sterilization; Nazi Holocaust refugees of the mid-1940s. When members of these groups or their descendants pick up guns and fulfill their army service, they become implicated in a particular way in settler colonization. Nevertheless, these groups have mutable relationships with the colonial state and thus mercurial interactions with the Palestinians. Working through these entanglements will be of great benefit to the future of Israel/Palestine.

Returning to the American landscape, some folks are deeply implicated as settlers while others do not overtly enact colonization, but it is not contradictory to observe that all nonblacks and non-Natives are morally implicated in U.S. and Canadian colonization—at least in the sense of bearing a moral obligation to end it. In this framework, the location of U.S.- and Canada-based Palestine solidarity work assumes tremendous importance. Palestinians and their allies in America have done strong work engaging cross-ethnic organizing, but they must consistently take initiative rather than waiting for overtures of Native solidarity. This kind of initiative can reverberate across the Atlantic: acknowledging a mutual obligation as settlers offers a terrific basis for Jewish–Arab organizing that elides the raw psychological power of the Holy Land. Investment in projects of American decolonization foregrounds a disciplined commitment to justice in Palestine.

What does it mean for multiethnic communities to devote themselves to the cessation (or reversal) of Israeli colonization when they conduct work in spaces that are themselves colonized? There is no singular answer, but raising the question constitutes an important purchase of consciousness. In *Uncivil Rites: Palestine and the Limits of Academic Freedom*, I consider the question in an autobiographical reflection, recalling my family's position as immigrants in cultures of race and belonging that nearly erased Indigenous peoples. All immigrants of color have such experiential possibilities, but they need to be actualized through the difficult work of demythologizing the narratives of U.S. industriousness and color-blind merit. There can be no philosophical transition to inter/nationalism without a rejection of the self-confident rhetoric that conceptualizes American history as settled and thus immune to the reversals of nationalist insurgency.

Inter/nationalism can effectively contravene this inveterate rhetoric once it has been identified and anatomized. Inter/nationalism in turn urges a retreat from the industrial economies of the neoliberal state and demands focus on Indigenist notions of cultural and ecological sustainability. More than anything, it requires advocates of Palestine solidarity in the United States and Canada to divest themselves from the false promises of manifest destiny and turn their attention to extracting themselves from complicity, however tenuous it may seem, in forms of colonization they deplore when practiced by Israel. Doing so is not simply a matter of proclaiming support for Natives, but incorporating that support into material and intellectual action. In order to accomplish this goal, it is necessary to examine some key tenets of American Indian and Indigenous theory.

Decolonizing America

American Indian and Indigenous theory, if we can even put forward such a category, does not follow any particular formula. (I do not mean to imply that there is no such thing as American Indian and Indigenous theory; instead, I want to indicate that it is not nearly as hermetic as the terminology might indicate.) Qualifying under the rubric of "theory" is any analysis that treats the structural conditions of economy, governance, culture, identity, violence, or discourse. Palestine solidarity has much to gain by studying Native theorists. Once thus educated, it will have more to contribute.

American Indian and Indigenous theory is wide-ranging. I am concerned with the aspects of that theory invested in questions of inter/nationalism. In studying these areas of theory, one notices, despite tremendous philosophical and methodological variation, some consistent themes:

- A devotion to centering Indigenous peoples within their own points of view.

- Emphasis on the destructiveness of a globalized elite that facilitates plutocracy (and emphasis on class and international capital more generally).

- Engagement with various forms of racial analysis in both popular and scholarly writing.

- Reorganization of static, and statist, notions of kinship, belonging, and citizenship (legal, discursive, and cultural).

- Discrete understandings of Indigenist politics shaded against but in conversation with Marxism, anarchism, postcolonialism, and other traditions of the global Left.

- A desire to recover or rethink gender roles and sexuality in both community and academic settings.

- Recognition of the importance of theory with material uses.

- Unwavering belief in the importance of survivance and a corresponding dedication to the well-being of The People.

In his magisterial *Red Skin, White Masks,* Glen Coulthard explores each of these themes. He declares, "Native thinkers and leaders are coming on the scene intent on changing things, entirely. With the last stores of our patience, Native writers, musicians, and philosophers are trying to explain to settlers that their values and the true facts of their existence are at great odds, and that the Native can never be completely erased or totally assimilated."[7] Coulthard leverages this plainspoken declaration into a treatise on the failure of the liberal state (Canada, specifically) to accommodate Native demands for autonomy, though the concept of autonomy in Coulthard's usage is explicitly liberationist. Indeed, he argues passionately for a rejection of the framework of recognition as a solution to continued Native dispossession and an extrication of Native polities and political identities from that framework.

Coulthard offers an analysis of class and cultural politics that exceeds in range and intensity recent studies that address comparable issues, but his overarching critique is in keeping with trends in American Indian and Indigenous studies. Coulthard organizes them into complex assessments of Indigenous peoplehood entrapped by the systematic iniquities of modernity, often through the practice of neocolonialism. We see in this type of approach a profound concern with global economies of neoliberalism, imperialism, and patriarchy even in a context of profoundly local approaches. A consistent theme of these approaches is the idea of discrete national communities as global agents in dialogue with forces of transnational commerce. I do not squeeze this theory into an inter/nationalist paradigm, but employ the term "inter/nationalism" in order to name an extant phenomenon.

Penelope Kelsey argues "for a gathering together of the many threads that constitute tribal identity as part of Indigenous imaginings of nationhood."[8] We see again the specificity of autochthonous nations envisioned as part of a global context. Kelsey contemplates "how we might theorize Indigenous nationalisms that respond to postcontact complexities of community formation while de-emphasizing settler definitions of identity that have infiltrated current understandings of Indigenous nationhood and sovereignty."[9] Her use of the verb *infiltrated* intimates that settler definitions of identity consciously overwhelm the Indigenous and that less compromised understandings of Indignety are recoverable. She does not endeavor to eliminate but to de-emphasize those settler definitions, a move that grants a certain permanence to the epistemologies of settlement and asks for methodologies devoid of nostalgia in return. These matters are best accomplished, she argues, across national boundaries.

Audra Simpson's *Mohawk Interruptus* provides a useful complement to *Red Skins, White Masks*. Simpson examines the Kahnawà:ke Mohawk as a specific national community that nonetheless offers insight into conflicts and tensions besetting Native nations around the continent. The book's subtitle, *Life across the Borders of Settler States,* points to inter/national theorization, the word *life* signaling multitextured concerns. Simpson undermines numerous colonial shibboleths around citizenship, recognition, and sovereignty, and reorganizes those concepts around Indigenous personhood and community. There is no way to reduce her argument to a singular thesis; she examines a centuries-long Haudenosaunee (and, more broadly, Native) rejection of incorporation into cultural and juridical paradigms of the colonial nation-state. To reject those nation-states, Simpson illustrates, is an assertion of sovereignty as a basal form of cultural and political identity.

Of particular interest to my project is Simpson's formulation around the physical and symbolic documents of Mohawk independence:

> If a Haudenosaunee person is to travel internationally . . . on a [Haudenosaunee] Confederacy passport, then the very boundaries and lawfulness of the original territorial referent is called into question. The entire United States may then be "international," which, some would argue, it was prior to contact and still is. Like Indigenous bodies, Indigenous sovereignties and Indigenous political orders prevail within and apart from settler governance. This form of "nested sovereignty" has implications for the sturdiness of nation-states over all, but especially for formulations of political membership as articulated and fought over within these nested sovereignties.[10]

Simpson offers a startling amount of intellectual material in this passage. I am most interested in her use of the terms "international" and "nested." She implies that the liberal state is not as sturdy as its mythologies indicate, in large part because Indigenous peoples are nested within their boundaries in ways that dislodge statist jurisdiction. The industrialized North American nation-state is not unified in its own administration and cannot therefore be named as ascendant. It is international not only in imperial commitment, but also within its internal composition.

Simpson juxtaposes this form of internationalism with Mohawk inter/nationalism, which precedes and modifies the Canadian and U.S. entities. Her supposition that the land now known as Canada and the United States was international (which I render inter/national) before European contact illuminates a kind of cultural and discursive commerce that offers considerable opportunity for dialogue. The commerce is also physical. Inter/nationalism entails the transit of bodies—"transit" is a term put to excellent use, we might recall, by Jodi Byrd in *The Transit of Empire*—as well as the right to travel with the documents of one's choosing. This right is not simply a matter of claiming national belonging or performing sovereignty, but also a rejection of colonial jurisdiction. Similar actions, symbolic and tangible, occur throughout the world, a collective project to conceptualize different ways of existing as citizens in the nested spaces of self-determination.

The global dynamics of Simpson's analysis resonate in much recent scholarship. Chadwick Allen, for instance, assesses these possibilities using the term "trans-Indigenous" (like much of his work, mainly in relation to American Indians and Maoris). He writes: "Whether mourned as loss or celebrated as survivance, the realities of contemporary Indigenous identities describe multiple kinds of diversity and complexity; often, they describe seeming paradoxes of simultaneity, contradiction, coexistence. These qualities are the contemporary Indigenous norm rather than its tragic exception."[11] The norm Allen identifies can function as something of an aggregated disaggregation, from which his notion of the "trans-Indigenous" derives much of its meaning. I have no desire to bicker over fine-tuned grammatical algorithms. "Trans-Indigenous" is an excellent term for cross-border scholarship, particularly as a disruption of static uses of the preposition *across*. I prefer "inter/nationalism" not because I reject Allen's analysis or methodology, but because it better describes a set of issues with which I am concerned. Those issues overlap with the themes in Allen's book, but they are not identical. I engage *Trans-Indigenous* as a way to usefully diagnose these distinctions. The goal is to fully consider the benefits and drawbacks of these global approaches.

I position inter/nationalism in a slightly different space than trans-Indigenous, though they share considerable intellectual territory. Inter/nationalism is more explicitly trained on the discourses and practices of political organizing while trans-Indigeneity largely is a critical methodology for the study of literature and culture. Yet Allen devotes plenty of space to the material realities of Indigenous communities and I certainly do not ignore the production and reception of literature. The predominance of "nationalism" in my formulation highlights liberatory elements of decolonization, in which the arts and literature play a significant role. "Inter" intimates a grounded set of mutual relationships while "trans" points to phenomena uncontained by geopolitical strictures. Allen's observation that those phenomena are inevitable, even if some folks consider them undesirable, locates American Indian and Indigenous studies in distinct nations even as it disencumbers them from the dissonance of modernity.

Patrick Wolfe provides productive complements to Coulthard, Simpson, Kelsey, and Allen. In "Settler Colonialism and the Elimination of the Native," Wolfe suggests that "settler colonialism does not simply replace native society tout court. Rather, the process of replacement maintains the refractory imprint of the native counterclaim."[12] Here a dialectic of Indigenous resistance and colonial domination produces unsettled histories on disputed geographies. Wolfe later notes that "Settler colonialism was foundational to modernity. Frontier individuals' endless appeals for state protection not only presupposed a commonality between the private and official realms. In most cases (Queensland was a partial exception), it also presupposed a global chain of command linking remote colonial frontiers to the metropolis."[13] Wolfe shows how the particulars of Israeli colonization arise from long-standing strategies of foreign settlement on other continents, conditioned by the European metropoles from which Zionism emerged. The very fact of colonization's inability to replace the native produces the conditions of inter/nationalism. The colonizer's desire to create a new man in a new world relies on mythologized landscapes isolated from any possibility of native agency. A crucial element of native agency exists in the desire so ably illuminated by Coulthard to speak clearly about the injustice and unsustainability of conquest.

Taken together (though they are far from identical), the pieces I cite, along with the broader theoretical context in which they exist, demand the primacy of Indigenous perspectives, but also recognize the global economies of Indigenous dispossession. The possibilities of Indigenous liberation are indivisible from that recognition, which entails analysis of class, race, gender, culture, sexuality, and governance. Inveterate focus on one's immediate national community still exists and remains a necessary feature of decolonization, but inter/national approaches have shown themselves capable of benefiting local priorities.

I do not want to wander too deeply into the moral and methodological preferences of Native scholars. My reflections in the previous paragraph are most germane in relation to Palestine, an example of the indispensability of Native theory to Palestinian decolonization. As Keith Feldman, Alex Lubin, Sunaina Maira, Nadine Naber, Edward Said, and many others illustrate, Palestine has long entailed international and inter/national perspectives. The main question confronting us is how to optimize those perspectives in relation to the multivalent labor of Palestine solidarity.

Palestine in the World

In the introduction and first chapter, I raise the notion of a Palestine disaggregated from its own geography. To provide more heft to that notion, we can engage the work of John Collins and Mark Rifkin. Their work deploys and assesses inter/national phenomena vis-à-vis Palestine, but each scholar raises his analysis in a distinct framework whose complementary structures offer useful analytic possibilities.

Collins mainly is concerned with "a Palestine that is globalized and a globe that is becoming Palestinized," a formulation, through the verb *becoming,* that accepts Palestine's globalization while conceding that the globe's Palestinization is incomplete.[14] He attributes this dialectic between Palestine and the globe to a handful of factors: the "new historians" in Israel who (belatedly) exposed the state's founding mythologies; the work of Palestinian writers in proffering transnational connections; the strength of Palestinian culture in diaspora; "the global flow of the technologies of violence";[15] developments in worldwide media (including social media); and the importance of Palestine to the populations of many countries. (I would add BDS to Collins's list.) Plus, Collins notes, modern Palestine has always been functionally globalized, colonized by the Ottomans and the British and then falling victim to a settlement project profoundly international in nature.

For Collins, these developments would have been impossible were it not for worldwide skepticism about Israel's self-image as exceptionally humane. This self-image effectively juxtaposes Israel with the divine immanence of U.S. nationhood (and, to a lesser degree, with other colonial ventures). Dislodging Israel from its self-image requires concomitant assessment of a set of historical narratives from which the idea of the Zionist state emerged. Collins asks us to consider an international Palestine not merely from the point of view of liberatory agitation, particularly throughout the Southern Hemisphere, but also in conjunction with the considerable global capital invested in Israeli colonization. He claims that Palestine has

> emerged as a focus of attention for activists connected with the broader global justice movement that has targeted a whole range of hierarchical, undemocratic and predatory structures associated with global capitalism and US imperialism. The most recent US Social Forum, for example, held in Detroit in June 2010, featured an entire program devoted to Palestine including a "People's Movement Assembly," multiple workshops, cultural events and a solidarity mural.[16]

This passage might appear to conceptualize global Palestine as an extraordinary phenomenon, but in reality Collins treats it as an inevitable feature of innate forces governing world politics: capitalism, imperialism, colonization, trade, technology, militarism. Palestine, then, is not exceptional. That self-image belongs to the Israeli colonizer. The fact that Palestine is understandable as a palimpsest of prior (and concurrent) episodes of settler colonialism makes it all the easier (and more necessary) to understand within the framework of our actual world rather than the ethereal teleology of self-mythologies.

Mark Rifkin, whose wide-ranging work on Indigenous peoples exhibits inter/national commitments, recently turned his attention to Israel/Palestine. That turn has resulted in a creative approach to a well-worn topic. He does so by reassessing two terms common in discussion of Zionism and Palestine solidarity:

> When these concepts—apartheid and settler colonialism—are treated as if they referred to the same thing, which they often are within scholarly accounts of Israel/Palestine, the notion of indigeneity tends to vanish, in that the political goal for Indigenous peoples gets envisioned as full belonging within the nation-state rather than as acknowledgment of their distinct modes of sovereignty and self-definition. That process of conceptual collapse, which I will address in this essay, significantly truncates the meaning of Indigenous self-determination in ways that not only have implications for thinking Palestinian peoplehood(s) but for engaging Indigenous peoplehoods more broadly, given the ways that the case of Israel/Palestine (like that of South Africa before it) itself transits transnationally and comes to serve as a prism through which to view other political struggles.[17]

The distinction between "apartheid" and "settler colonialism," in Rifkin's reckoning, is far more than semantic. "Apartheid" tacitly supersedes "settler colonialism," which in turn prevents serious understanding of Israel's history or of its present behavior. In Rifkin's language, Indigeneity "goes missing" when we use the frame of apartheid, despite the fact that Israel and apartheid South Africa share important features.

Rifkin later argues, "In contrast to the narrative of apartheid as an institutionalized racial cleavage within citizenship, settler colonialism names the imposition of the state over top of existing peoples, whose prior presence makes them Indigenous." This notion of the "Indigenous" coheres to my sense of the term vis-à-vis Palestine. Rifkin does not base Indigeneity in Palestine on historical narratives or rights-based paradigms, but on precolonial inhabitance. More specifically, this model of Indigeneity does not distinguish between Jew and Arab; the distinction exists between Israeli settler and pre-Zionist denizen. Viewpoints that raise Israel–Palestine in an apartheid setting elide, even if unintentionally, a proper focus on garrison colonization, though apartheid illuminates significant elements of the so-called conflict. Rifkin is less interested in convincing readers to disavow an apartheid frame altogether than he is in centering settler colonization as the foundation of Israel's very existence.

To develop this argument, Rifkin points out that

> [w]ith respect to Israel, this dynamic characterizes not only the invasion and occupation of the lands seized in 1967 but the campaign of institutionalized terror and ethnic cleansing (al-Nakba) through which the state was founded; the continuous programs of "transfer" and displacement within 1948 borders; the demolition of legally unrecognized Palestinian houses and villages in the Occupied Territories and pre-1967 borders; the deferral of any substantive Palestinian governmental authority over lands claimed by Israel; the denial of, or highly constricted access to, vital resources, such as water; and the denial of the ability of exiled Palestinians to return for fear they will reclaim their lands.

This critique of the Israeli state lends itself to emphasis on sovereignty and self-determination as analytic (and political) categories. To accept Rifkin's critique is to reject long-standing claims of Israel's "right to exist." The act of rejection is not of great consequence, however. More critical is the reframing of the Palestinians' claims to inhabitation on ancestral land from one of demography to ontology. Those claims to inhabitation encompass a range of demands in keeping with the imperatives of Indigenous peoples throughout the globe: autonomy, sovereignty, self-determination, stewardship.

The perspective Rifkin employs is not new, but it is novel. Palestinians have long attempted (with some success) to raise claims as an Indigenous people in both legal and discursive capacities. Rifkin seeks an imaginative shift among those invested in Palestinian decolonization. By situating Palestinians as subjects of a contested geography and not victims of limited access based on biology or ethnicity, Rifkin puts Palestine in conversation with worldwide settler colonialism. Here it allows the dimensions of Zionist messianism and exceptionalism to become more recognizable and thus quite a bit less messianistic and exceptional than it would like the world to accept.

I read Collins and Rifkin together because Rifkin enacts Collins's notion of a global Palestine within a precise context of inter/nationalism. We see in both authors' arguments how Palestine can be imaginative: imagined in creative ways and also constitutive of a worldly imagination. These imaginative possibilities are essential to any understanding of American Indian studies and Palestine solidarity.

The New Comparisons

Let us survey a few noteworthy interactions between Native and Palestinian decolonization, though what follows is not exhaustive. These interactions occupy two broad categories: organizing alliances and discursive connections.

Perhaps both categories prevail in a 2015 art exhibition titled *The Map Is Not the Territory,* which examines the "parallel paths" of Palestinians, Native Americans, and Irish. The touring exhibition made its way around the United States and the United Kingdom. Curated by Jennifer Heath and Dagmar Painter, it "looks at relationships and commonalities in Palestinian, Native American and Irish experiences of invasion, occupation and colonization—not as novelty or polemic, but as history and current world events."[18] Comprised of painting, sketches, photography, and text, the exhibition offers three national artistic traditions in physical proximity. Heath and her collaborators sought a particular sort of political art, featuring artists who "confront history, investigate personal and political dialogue and reflect the multiple truths in Korzybski's dictum [that 'the map is not the territory']."[19] The art is self-consciously trained on the complex afterlives of colonization.

Of special interest are the spatial arrangements that exist around terms such as "map" and "territory" in conjunction with visual artifacts. Those artifacts are meant to represent sentient cultural traditions. The artistic objects are compelling on their own but even more powerful in conversation with their contemporaries. Overt articulations of Native, Palestinian, or Irish peoplehood are not self-contained. The exhibition features a fair amount of spatial and political transgression—an inter/national conception of "territory," if you will. Visual artists and producers of text work across the comparable cartographies of settler colonization. The most notable inter/national feature of the exhibition is its transit. Many art shows travel to different settings, but *The Map Is Not the Territory* was curated for that purpose. Its design rejects, perhaps undermines, the spatial restrictions of colonization. It seeks different audiences in disparate places, while binding those audiences to a common thematic frame. If we recall Jodi Byrd's creative uses of the term "transit" as something that identifies a constant movement of state power into new geographies, then it becomes easier to imagine the utility of decolonial art whose very display exists in transition.

It is with great surprise and pleasure that it is possible to connect *The Map Is Not the Territory* to the work of Gilles Deleuze. In 1984, Deleuze conducted a brief interview with Elias Sanbar, founder of the *Journal of Palestine Studies*. The interview, which quickly transforms into conversation, shows Deleuze to be a sharp political thinker. He begins the interview by observing, "Something seems to have ripened on the Palestinian side. A new tone, as if they have overcome the first state of their crisis, as if they have attained a region of certainty and serenity, of 'right' *(droit)*, which bears witness to a new consciousness. A state which allows them to speak in a new way, neither aggressively nor defensively, but 'equal to equal' with everyone."[20] The interview occurred well before the initiation of a formal peace process, so Deleuze does not speak necessarily of material gains but of an ontological presence in Israel and the West that had long been cleansed of Palestine's existence. His formulation "the first state of their crisis" implies that future crises will happen or that an extant crisis has yet to culminate. The ripening of Palestine, then, portends changes of an indeterminate nature.

In order to provide concrete possibilities, Deleuze contextualizes his analysis by turning to American history. Noting that Sanbar insists "on the comparison with American Indians," Deleuze suggests,

> There are two very different movements within capitalism. Now it is a matter of taking a people on their own territory and making them work, exploiting them, in order to accumulate a surplus: that's what is ordinarily called a colony. Now, on the contrary, it is a matter of emptying a territory of its people in order to make a leap forward, even if it means making them into a workforce elsewhere. The history of Zionism and Israel, like that of America, happened that second way: how to make an empty space, how to throw out a people?[21]

Preceding this passage is the strange claim that "the Palestinians are not in the situation of colonized peoples but of evacuees, of people driven out," a condition Deleuze also ascribes to Natives.

It is difficult to cosign Deleuze's observation, for Natives and Palestinians fit the dynamics of colonized societies according to every conceivable criterion. Natives, for instance, do not exist simply in exile, but also on ancestral land bases subsumed by both U.S. jurisdiction and capital. Palestinians too inhabit this condition, especially in the Occupied Territories, though many have made compelling arguments that Palestinian citizens of Israel are similarly colonized.[22] We might grant that Deleuze speaks of colonial desire, distinguishing the United States' and Israel's ethnic cleansing projects from, say, the transatlantic slave trade or King Leopold's conquest of the Congo, which necessitated a surplus of subjected labor. In this sense, he is mostly correct: the United States and Israel desired uninhabited land, in keeping with a particular biblical mythos constitutive of the virginal landscape that racial violence was tasked to produce in the absence of the barrenness both colonies so forcefully hypothesized. Neither colony, however, fully declaimed the utility of native labor—both, in fact, often relied on it. Therefore, while colonization in America and Palestine looks significantly different than in South Asia or Indochina, capitalist strictures do not allow for the sort of tidy bifurcation Deleuze proposes.

Sanbar's response is unsurprising: "We are . . . the American Indians of the Jewish settlers in Palestine. In their eyes our one and only role consisted in disappearing. In this it is certain that the history of the establishment of Israel reproduces the process which gave birth to the United States of America."[23] He does not fully agree with Deleuze, though the disagreement is implicit. Whereas Deleuze speaks of material consequences, Sanbar examines mental phenomena: "In order to succeed, the emptiness of the terrain must be based in an evacuation of the 'other' from the settlers' own heads."[24] Sanbar's distinction between physical and psychological disappearance is crucial. It allows for an accommodation of global colonial paradigms that Deleuze's analysis forestalls. The imaginaries of settlement factor into those paradigms in ways that supersede mere class interest (though they are always attached). Yet, even here Sanbar limits his scope to foundational settler ideologies. Neither Natives nor Palestinians were erased from the colonial imagination; both were critical to the colonizer's ability to imagine a new identity. For Natives and Palestinians, the presence of settlers is inescapable, but the settler can never escape his own erasures. He is constituted precisely by what he wishes to expunge.

The Deleuze–Sanbar conversation is useful for what it illuminates about its own historical moment and in revealing how far inter/national critique has developed in the past thirty-five years. Deleuze and Sanbar did not have the benefit of a huge body of Native scholarship—certainly not of the magnitude that now exists. In recent years, comparisons of the type they proffer do better at recognizing the ongoing nature of U.S. and Canadian colonization and are thus better able to relate the conditions of Native life to Palestine. Let us peruse a few examples.

A good starting point is a 2002 essay by Gyasi Ross in the *Progressive*. Discounting (though not rejecting) a sense of kinship with Palestinians based on mutual displacement and Indigeneity, Ross explains that "this fraternal feeling for my brothers and sisters in Gaza and on the West Bank is due to a much more basic and primal feeling of fear: the realization that what befalls one oppressed group inevitably befalls others."[25] Here a notion of historical symmetry guides Ross's interest in Palestine. He expresses interest in disrupting violence that long precedes Zionism: "My sense of kinship with Palestinian people thus comes from a reminder of my own people's suffering, and from an interest in stopping such suffering from happening ever again."[26] Invoking the "genocidal atrocities" of U.S. colonization, Ross declares that "every person who strives for humanity also has a strong interest in preventing those same atrocities from occurring in another place at another time to another group of people—in this particular situation, to the Palestinians."[27]

This argument avoids the sort of theoretical heft we see in the Deleuze–Sanbar conversation or the eager articulations of kinship evident in *The Map Is Not the Territory,* but it presents an ethical point of view common to inter/national discourse: suffering is never local. It is a helpful point of view in light of the material relationships among settler-colonial states. Chronicling a long list of Canadian government crimes against Indigenous communities, performed under the aegis of neoliberal marketeering, James Cairns concludes, "So while settler colonialism in Canada has always been about the violent displacement of indigenous peoples, the Harper government's passionate defence of Israel and attacks on opposition to Israeli apartheid is also connected to its determination to defeat resistance to its agenda, at home and abroad. Canada not only supports but partners with and profits from Israel's domination of Palestine."[28] The impetus for a Western head of state to support Israel surpasses geopolitical convenience. It is a question of neoliberal economy that binds support of Israel to a constellation of regressive global policies—and to an image of history that is not actually historical.

In 2013, journalist Max Blumenthal attended the Aspen Summit, a gathering of policy and military officials moderated by CNN anchor Wolf Blitzer. One of the speakers, recently retired CENTCOM (Central Command) chief General James Mattis, proclaimed that the "war on terror" is of indeterminate length, like "the constant skirmishing between [the U.S. cavalry] and the Indians" during the nineteenth century.[29] Blumenthal reports a disturbing array of what he calls "extermination fantasies," with participants speaking openly of "smoking" and "killing" people in the Southern Hemisphere. Mattis's invocation of the Indian wars is of a piece with the nomenclature of American weaponry—Chinook, Apache, Black Hawk, Lakota, Kiowa, Creek, and Cayuse helicopters, Huron transportation aircraft, and Tomahawk cruise missiles, not to mention the common reference to enemy territory as "Indian country"—and recapitulates well-worn notions of civilizational as well as geographic conflict.

Mattis did not deploy a metaphor—or, perhaps we can say he was not solely being metaphorical. He shared a distinctive vision of the United States' role in the world, one derived from the messianism of an engagement with Natives containing no beginning or end. The extermination fantasies Blumenthal witnessed are not just an extension of prior colonial practice or the habitual vocabulary of an imperium but an understanding of exceptional achievement animated and renewed by the logic of conquest. That the United States is fundamentally a stranger to both geographies only adds power to the achievement's mystique.

Yet there is almost always a critical omission in these narratives. Like so many before him, Mattis imagines some abstruse end point to the Indian wars, though judging by the healthy state of Native nationalisms the history he takes for granted is not quite settled. Take this declaration from Knesset member Miri Regev, in response to the accusation that she wants to transfer an entire population (the Palestinian Bedouin of the Naqab Desert): "Yes, as the Americans did to the Indians."[30] I spent time with this sort of formulation in chapter 1, so I do not want to repeat myself. Let us then consider Regev's analogy as a historical fragment—that is, as a rhetorical device that misreads history in order to buttress the conduct of injustice in the present. We can begin with tense: Regev approves of what Americans *did* to the Indians. In her mind, the doing is evidently done. She forecloses, or at least ignores, the possibility that Americans still do stuff to "the Indians."

Regev inhabits two myths. Only one of those myths helps her cause, which is to invoke the permanent victories of American history in order to justify the desire for a comparable outcome in Israel. This myth might be called the discourse of divine fulfillment. We have thus far covered it in some detail. The other myth she inhabits is that of a suprahistorical existence for Natives, who are not agents in the push and pull of Americana, but an absence to be periodically marched across a stage of diplomatic grandiosity. There is much analytic potential in recognition of the second myth. It can act as a basis to debunk the discourse of divine fulfillment and expose the tenuous philosophical edifice upon which settler colonization proceeds. We might say that the increasing ubiquity of this myth reveals just how profoundly the settler colony relies on material advantages in the absence of moral or discursive heft.

It is not an easy myth to unravel, but the attempt is worthwhile. When Regev and others use Native dispossession to rationalize the colonization of Palestine, they center the settler as the only worthwhile historical actor in dialectics of geopolitical violence. However, they overlook the impossibility of total victory because they are incapable of ascribing normal human impulses to the native, despite so much evidence to the contrary. (Compare, for example, Regev's fantasy of the expendable indigene with Ze'ev Jabotinsky's hard-boiled realism.) In turn, they entrap themselves in the same structural limits by which they are constituted. The invocation of Natives as a justification of Palestinian dispossession in fact acts as an endorsement of continued Palestinian resistance. Regev and fellow ethnonationalists are not the only ones to juxtapose a Native past with a Palestinian future for the sake of rhetorical persuasion. It happens sometimes within the Palestine solidarity community. While there is appeal in positioning a misunderstood Palestine amid a tragic history with which many Americans are at least abstractly familiar, this familiarity belongs to the realm of mythology. As such, it enlivens the death of the Native subject. Palestine solidarity activists, even with the best of intentions, ought to assiduously avoid this formulation.

For example, activist Moe Diab, who does excellent, invaluable work, noted in 2013 as Israel contemplated the infamous Prawer Plan, which was to displace numerous Bedouin from ancestral lands: "The international community must increase pressure on the government of Israel to reverse this racial discriminatory plan, which violates International Humanitarian Law and Human Rights Law, before its [sic] too late and this goes down as another Native American–like tragedy in history. We must stop it now before our kids are reading about the ethnic cleansing and destruction of a native population and their once preserved culture and unique traditions."[31] In terms of its content, Diab's statement is comparable to Regev's. Their desires, not their appraisals, differ. I see no need to proffer a moral critique of those desires, as it detracts from less obvious but more important analytic possibilities.

It makes perfect sense for Diab to fret over the fate of Palestinian tribespeople facing state-sanctioned displacement. The destruction of numerous Native nations is an obvious and attractive corollary. That Diab references it is no surprise; it is the context of the logic that is troublesome. If we recall that in numerous cases Native nations have been the victors in conflict with settlers and that conflict of some variety remains a crucial feature of both Native and U.S. governance, then the analogy does not work for two reasons: (1) it misreads the existing interplay of American governance and Native nationalism; and (2) it implies that displacement of Palestinian Bedouin would be permanent based on tacit acceptance of the settler's linear induction. To concede permanence to a settler state's legislative or ideological violence reinforces, if only implicitly, the settler state's self-appointed authority. We can avoid this problem at a moral or rhetorical level by ameliorating the temporal disjunctions of any comparison of Natives and Palestinians: Natives are not a defeated precursor to impending Palestinian dispossession but contemporaneous agents who directly inform the conditions of Palestine, just as Palestinians directly inform the conditions of Indian country.

Palestine solidarity does little service to Native peoples by reifying U.S. history as the petrified underpinning of an Israeli resurrection. Our conceptions of colonization and decolonization should be more dynamic and more attuned to the possibilities of unconventional wisdom. The alliances increasingly formed among Native and Palestinian scholars, activists, and civic groups make clear the impossibility of Native defeat. To even acknowledge the existence of Natives is to accept that they were not defeated. Palestinians are way too familiar with the pain of an unacknowledged existence to ever consciously withhold that sort of acknowledgment.

American Indian Studies and Palestine Solidarity

Finally, we arrive at the question of American Indian studies and Palestine solidarity. (We actually have engaged the question throughout this chapter, just not explicitly.) A quotation in Al Jazeera from former Ardoch Algonquin Chief Robert Lovelace moves us in a good direction:

> Colonialism is a worldwide scourge. It has been going on for hundreds of years. And the outcomes are now hitting really full force: the poverty, the displaced people, the migrants. It's time for all aboriginal people to stand up and to recognise that our liberation, our freedom and our justice are tied together with all the peoples in the world who are oppressed, whether they live in Mexico, or Latin America, the United States, or in Africa or in the Middle East or in the Far East.[32]

The quote is strong, if not earth-shattering. The setting from which Lovelace spoke underscores its power: Messina, a port city in Sicily, moments before he boarded a flotilla headed to the Gaza Strip in June 2015 in order to break a long and crushing Israeli siege. The location of the comment matters because Lovelace deployed it as a mission statement, not simply a proposition.

In describing his motivation for joining the Freedom Flotilla, a journey fraught with the possibility of harm or even death, Lovelace chose to underscore a worldly politics rather than solely fixating on Palestine. He thus viewed his act of resistance as one that has consequences for Indigenous peoples on numerous continents, which can only be the case if the evolution or resolution of the Palestinian struggle has far-reaching consequences, a point few would contest. Because few would contest this point, we can identify an extant basis for inter/national paradigms vis-à-vis the work of Palestine solidarity. Lovelace stepped onto the flotilla in order to participate in a dangerous act of civil disobedience against a murderous Israeli regime.

American Indian studies should be important to Palestine solidarity, then, because it encompasses a world whose deep concern for the well-being of Palestinians illuminates the geographies to which our ideas and actions must travel in order for our minds and bodies to achieve liberation. Moreover, the articulations of Palestine solidarity that occur in America are already embroiled in local politics, if only unconsciously, and are therefore obligated by ethics and efficacy to analyze the conditions of state power in relation to the Native nations on whose lands that solidarity occurs. Finally, the turn to inter/national paradigms in various theories of decolonization necessitates a corresponding internationalization of the so-called Holy Land, a recognition increasingly evident in the material and intellectual spaces of Palestine solidarity. Pertaining to the final point, at no time has theorization of America or Palestine been strictly provincial. I speak mainly of a body of work responsive to, and in many ways ahead of, the coagulation of power among a hermetic global elite. These days, decolonization seems extremely difficult, but it is quite easy to identify its targets. This relationship of easy identification with extreme difficulty is causal.

There are many ways to produce an analysis of American Indian studies in relation to Palestine solidarity, but, given the context of this project and my own professional location, I am most interested in scholarship and academic labor in the United States. Research and campus organizing centered on or concerned with Palestine have long produced transnational outcomes. We are at a point where enough is happening specifically around Natives and Indigenous peoples that it is possible to evaluate observable phenomena and think closely about the implications, pitfalls, and possibilities of growing inter/national strategies and methodologies. In academic settings, the precariousness of Palestine renders those possibilities more interesting. Palestine is precarious vis-à-vis its undesirability and its destabilizing potential. Conjoining it to American Indian studies maximizes the anxiety it induces among those guarding institutional respectability (as determined by neoliberal convention).

I propose five points to illustrate the importance of American Indian studies to Palestine solidarity:

1. As we saw in chapter 1, Palestine has already become important to American Indian studies. Reciprocity is essential because we have to account for the cartographies of its transit.

2. Important aspects of Palestine solidarity occur on land colonized by the United States or Canada. Just as the actions of diasporic Jewish communities in America influence the conduct of Israel, organizing around Palestine in American landscapes affects Palestinian nationalism. Both phenomena interact with Native politics. Acknowledging and assaying those interactions is an ethical imperative, not just a scholarly mandate.

3. Israel practices violence against people other than Palestinians. While Palestinians experience the lion's share of Zionist brutality, the brutal practices of Zionism have disturbed people around the globe, including in Indian country. Settler colonization does not belie tidy hierarchies but authorizes them. We need not reproduce those hierarchies. It is more useful to untangle the complexities of a dialogic ethnonationalism instead.

4. American Indian studies contains a long history of creative, insightful theorization around matters of great concern to Palestine solidarity: colonization, foreign settlement, self-determination, demography (including demographic manipulation), sovereignty, legal dispossession, messianic fervor, land claims, cultural recovery, repatriation, identity, citizenship, and representation.

5. The continued existence of Palestine as a global issue demands close analysis of specific comparative possibilities. We need not seek phenomena that are perfectly analogous, but material interactions that strongly correlate. For much of its modern history, Palestine has provided opportunities to examine correlations around the special relationship between the United States and Israel. These days, correlations are plentiful around matters of Native-Palestinian decolonization.

If we remember the examples I have provided of today's Indigenous theorization, then we can easily situate ourselves in an inter/national paradigm. The articulation of national aspirations in conjunction with a global focus specifies local forms of decolonization. Even the most hidebound national liberation movement must navigate issues beyond its dominant purview.

Palestine has eroded as a landscape or as a polity, but it has thrived as an idea, and as an ideal. This disparity informs a broader problem of the world, the maintenance of decolonial energy against violent market forces that constrict access to wealth, movement, resources, and citizenship. We can imagine better worlds, ones free of plutocracy and military occupation, but we possess too little material power to transform imagination into comprehensive results. This viewpoint is not defeatist. In contrast, it augurs a sort of hopefulness bordering on naïveté. It asks us to consider the practical usefulness of inter/national approaches in addition to their intellectual or imaginative value. The only salvageable things in this world are the futures we manage to keep alive. Our memories must therefore remain larger than the restraints of the colonizer's imagination. We have to create the world in which we intend to reside. That world, unlike the current one, must be amenable to our existence.

I reject forms of inter/nationalism that treat U.S. and Israeli colonialism as linear phenomena and that, as a result, conceptualize Palestine as a palimpsest of Native history. Serious engagement with American Indian studies quickly reveals this approach to be a bit too tidy and convenient. A major element of decolonization is undermining the tidiness and convenience of accepted wisdom. American Indian studies, like the communities it engages, is a living phenomenon that both precedes and portends the rites of conflict in Palestine. We can locate the dynamics of neoliberal governance within an understanding of Indigeneity to offset the dogmas of a New Left too often enamored of modernity. The point is to shift analysis from the industrialized world in the direction of Indigenous stewardship. Palestine has an important role to play in this project, as its intellectual history illustrates. Its relationship with American Indian and Indigenous studies will go a long way in determining its effective development as an inter/national avatar, one that works to liberate Native communities rather than visualizing them as artifacts of a tragic history.

I recall numerous conversations with friends who identify as Indigenous upon their return trips from Palestine. The overt cruelty of Israel's occupation inevitably stands out as something they find shocking and difficult to process. It is easy to see comparable colonial practices in America and Palestine—the style and location of colonies, state appropriation of resources, wildly divergent economic disbursements, the garrison nature of the settlers, the state's investment in a set of narrow mythologies—but the spatial dynamics and blatant security structures in Palestine register differently than they do in most cases in North America. Many Indigenous travelers to Palestine experience firsthand the ill-treatment of anybody who is not Jewish (as determined by the Israeli state). Those with dark skin enjoy special malignment. These visitors come closer than anybody to inhabiting the lived experience of a Palestinian, especially if we take into consideration the iterations of colonial suppression accumulated in their own nations.

These trips, often formal delegations, are now common. They provide an effective way for Palestinians to share the pain and joy of their lives with outsiders, who can live the culture of Palestine as guests, well fed and cared for meticulously. Most Palestinians of the Occupied Territories are barred from travel, so it is important that people of the world come to them (as difficult as Israel often makes it). The visuals of Israeli military occupation can be disconcerting. I know of nobody who has visited Palestine without returning deeply affected. One reason is that direct engagement with Palestine circumvents the mediating presence of U.S. corporate media. Another reason is that unless one manages extraordinary avoidance, the severe oppression of an entire people is everywhere visible. Severe oppression is everywhere visible in the United States as well, but it can be easy to miss if one conceptualizes American iniquity as a myth. In the end, the spatial dynamics of Palestine and the explicit trappings of racialized Israeli jurisprudence mark the geography of the Holy Land in ways that many find shocking. The resilience and good humor of Palestinians can also leave a profound impression on the visitor.

I raise these points—kind of a sanguine view of Palestinian society, of which I am profoundly fond—to illustrate that inter/nationalism need not be confined to the rarefied spaces of academic theorization. Nor do our conceptions of American Indian studies need to be confined to teaching and research. I have no gripe against theorization, or against teaching and research, but American Indian studies inhabits the same vastness of its eponymy. It includes Natives traveling to a colonized land across the ocean and being deeply moved and provoked by the experience. I doubt the need to convince the reader that Natives visiting Palestine is a noteworthy phenomenon for American Indian studies. What do those visits mean for Palestine solidarity? Here our analysis can take a number of useful forms; let us think about the question primarily as one of methodology.

If Indigenous peoples regularly visit Palestine and write moving pieces about their experiences, then it seems pretty obvious that the phenomenon is worth the attention of the academic fields devoted to the study of Palestine and the Palestinian people. What leads these people to Palestine? What do they see that affects them? Why are they so eager to connect those sights to their own experiences of colonization? How do those connections broaden or challenge how we think about Palestine as both a symbolic and a political geography?

We cannot properly address these questions without first engaging American Indian studies (and, preferably, Indigenous studies more broadly). In the field, we encounter dynamic analyses of cultural knowledge, history, political movements, jurisprudence, identity, and intellectual traditions. Many of those analyses look familiar to the advocate of Palestine solidarity; some of them are specific to a set of unique conditions. We further learn that the variability of belief and practice in Native communities makes comparison of viewpoints and ceremonies extremely difficult, likely impossible. (For example, while the intellectual class in most Indigenous communities is highly likely to sympathize with Palestinians, this sympathy might not exist as strongly among those representing different socioeconomic strata.) The basis of comparison exists within the architecture of inter/nationalism—its theorization, material emphases, and global decolonial imperatives. In other words, we are best served comparing for the sake of practicable forms of cross-cultural organizing, in recognition of the planetary nature of plutocratic and neoliberal dominion that maintains colonial structures.

I do not believe that the limitations of comparison actually limit our ability to evoke wide-ranging materials to compare. Nor do they forestall the possibilities of kinship among peoples who seem to have little in common beyond having been colonized. (The operative word is *seem*; communities share more in common than they differ, as a general rule.) When Robert Lovelace calls Gaza "the world's largest Indian reservation," he emphasizes possibilities of kinship in addition to proffering a comparative analysis.[33] Consider his perception of the Gaza Strip, which, by the physical standards of most Indian reservations, is tiny (twice the geographic area of Washington, D.C.). To call it the "largest" Indian reservation appears incongruous, unless we understand Lovelace to be deploying symbolism. Gaza is large in the world's imagination precisely because it is condensed into such a spectacular emblem of settler-colonial violence. Lovelace asks us to consider Gaza not as a place of mutual interest but as an articulation of a common history, one of concern to the Native even at a level of self-interest.

J. Kēhaulani Kauanui likewise speaks in terms more personal than mere geopolitics. Following a trip to Palestine, she reflected: "There's a particular Hawaiian connection for me when it comes to the question of Palestine. . . . I started to pursue that connection very seriously [in the mid-1990s] . . . and I've been pursuing those connections ever since."[34] Kauanui describes the participation of a Palestinian judge, Asma Khader, at the 1993 Hawaii International People's Tribunal; Khader's testimony deeply influenced the way Kauanui thinks about Palestine and Hawaii as corresponding sites of colonization. (Unlike with the majority of North American Indian nations, the U.S. colonization of Hawaii roughly coincides with the timeline of Zionism.) Her identification of a "particular" Hawaiian connection to Palestine highlights a personal investment that supersedes what many academics idealize as detached scholarship. Kauanui owns her attraction to Palestine based on her love of Hawaii.

It is another example of kinship in action—and a corresponding example of the desire of Indigenous scholars to improve the conditions of the communities from which they emerge (along with those they encounter along the way).

American Indian studies should be important to Palestine solidarity precisely because AIS accommodates this sort of personal investment. Too many Native scholars have called upon Palestine for us to consider the encounter an aberration or a passing fancy. More critically, the practice of Palestine solidarity in Native nations confers to advocates of Palestinian liberation a particular accountability to the well-being of those national communities. What does it mean to conduct the work of Palestine solidarity in spaces that are themselves still colonized? It means that our notions of decolonization should never treat Zionism as an isolated occupation; we have an opportunity to examine its earliest origin instead.

CONCLUSION
The Game of Our Time

■   ■   ■

In 1995, German company Catan released The Settlers of Catan, a board game rewarding strategy rather than luck. Catan is a mythical island whose settlers compete to exploit resources and develop public projects. Catan has no natives. By the time a typical game ends, though, Catan is a well-populated place featuring bustling cities and a free-market economy. Of the game, the *Washington Post* gushed, "Settlers of Catan is the board game of our time," noting that Facebook CEO Mark Zuckerberg plays with his girlfriend (now wife) and that the game embodies the spirit of Americana.[1] As of 2010, The Settlers of Catan had sold more than fifteen million units worldwide.

It inspired spin-offs, notably The Settlers of Canaan seven years later. The game uses the same concept, but a vastly different environment, this one based on an actual historical site and populated by real human beings (even if they are theologically imagined). According to Catan's marketing, "Each player represents a tribe of Israel as they seek to settle the land of Canaan. The time period of the game spans the time of Joshua's conquests of Canaan (Joshua), the turbulent years ruled by judges (Judges) through the choosing and crowning of King David (I & II Samuel)."[2] This period, if we are to believe the book on which the game is based, saw a handful of genocides. One of the strategies of The Settlers of Canaan is to build Jerusalem. The game requires no genocidal policy—it is more or less an

approximation of The Settlers of Catan—but the subtext of genocide is unavoidable. After all, the game reproduces Old Testament
epochs and celebrates the biblical vanquishment of pagan tribes.

Of course, recolonizing the Holy Land can become tedious, so
in 2010 Catan unveiled its latest spin-off, The Settlers of America.
The game's description: "As more and more settlers head west, new
cities pop up like mushrooms. Due to the distances between them,
these new cities quickly come to rely on new railroads for the trans-
port of vital goods. Trails become rails and create great wealth.
Soon, a complex railroad network develops, and steam belching
iron horses connect the thriving cities."[3] Players vie to earn miner-
als rights and access to new territories. An important aspect of the
game is generating Native support, a feature, perhaps because of
its mystical appeal, absent from The Settlers of Canaan. The game,
while acknowledging Natives, does not explicitly broach violence,
preferring, as in prior incarnations, to reward the strategic vision
of an industrious settler. The Settlers of America simulates actual
events, but asks players to conceptualize history anew, alluding to
pioneering mythologies while imagining a mythological reclamation project. The nineteenth century and imagery of the westward-
bound visionary predominate.

Catan has produced numerous settlement-themed games, but
two stand out because of named locations: Canaan and America.
There are many potential reasons. I suggest the following:

- The settlement of ancient Israel and the North American
  continent resonate deeply in the U.S. and European
  imagination.

- Affixing the gaming concept to actual histories, however
  tenuously, adds an element of excitement for potential
  consumers.

- Players might enjoy re-creating the heroic self-reference of
  their conquering identities.

- Game designers conceptualize the natives of Canaan and
  nineteenth-century America as fabulous creatures, not
  terribly unlike the fictive items of their other creations.

The final point is of particular importance. Gamers can play settler with the belief that settlement is history and thus the native, like the pioneer, no longer exists. The settler and the native in both games are fanciful props, but the settler's ultimate victory provides an impression of real life. The fantasy relies on encoded histories of actual colonization. As in any first-class American or Israeli education, the gamer gets to reinforce his sense of belonging on native land without the fuss of guilt or self-reflection.

The biblical overtones of The Settlers of Canaan extend to The Settlers of America. It is easy for players to render the Holy Land tribes obsolete; after all, those tribes play the role of vanquished in a foundational story of U.S. exceptionalism. Nobody these days identifies as a Canaanite or Hittite, at least not without irony. Millions of people, however, continue to identify as Native American, the same characters dispossessed in a board game enjoyed by techies and venture capitalists. Players do not understand Natives to be subjects of the present, though. If they did, playing The Settlers of America would be nearly impossible. Its appeal is the reproduction of an era in which Natives were vanquished. In this sense, it is profoundly similar to both The Settlers of Catan and The Settlers of Canaan.

Real histories can be subsumed by their own legendary effects on modernity, but their disappearance into the settler's overactive imagination is never complete. Even the archaic identifier "Canaanite" has currency among those who identify as Palestinian. The same is true, in slightly different ways, among those who identify as Israeli. Many Zionist narratives recycle the stories that are said to be biblical taproots of Western civilization. Even the doggedly modern cannot avoid the power of myth. In the myths of U.S. and Israeli nation building, the natives are everywhere absent. Distinctions of time dissipate. The destruction of Canaan may as well have happened the other day and the settlement of America is but the detritus of antiquity.

I confess: I do not even like board games. I probably have not played one in twenty years. Why, then, discuss the Catan suite of settlement adventures? Because it exemplifies the miasmic contradictions of settler colonization and the degree to which Holy Land mythologies inform the persistence of U.S. manifest destiny and its capitalist corollaries. If something can be played as a form of recreation, then it has clearly entered into the realm of imagination. If the thing being played happens to involve living histories and live human beings, then its imaginaries supersede the burdens of ethical deliberation. The *Washington Post* is correct to call The Settlers of Catan the game of our time—only it is not truly of our time, but a reflection of how we simultaneously adore and disavow the foundational stories of modernity. The Settlers of Catan/ Canaan/America is of a time that is still active, but pretends to be extinct.

The present American zeitgeist testifies to this disjunction (which is not really disjointed in the framework of settler logic). So many U.S. passions reenact the glories of nation building and consign Natives to the immobility of product labels and pithy signposts. Folks in the United States see Natives everywhere but the spaces in which they may be understood as living.

There is, of course, another lesson here, so obvious that I hesitate to mention it: you can play it on an endless repeat, and win at it with vim and gusto, assiduously following all the instructions, but it will never change the fact that colonization is not a game. Natives and Palestinians certainly are not making a game of decolonization, though they damn well intend to win.

ACKNOWLEDGMENTS

■　■　　■

For their feedback, either to the manuscript or to portions of it presented at public lectures, I am much indebted to Ashon Crawley, Vicente Diaz, Nick Estes, Keith Feldman, J. Kēhaulani Kauanui, Alex Lubin, Janet McAdams, Jeani O'Brien, Mark Rifkin, and Matthew Shenoda.

My thanks to Robert Warrior for including this book in the Indigenous Americas series and to Jason Weidemann of the University of Minnesota Press for his superb editorship.

Diana always sees me through the broodiness of writing projects with love and humor. I am blessed to be her partner.

NOTES

■   ■   ■

Introduction

1. Ward Churchill has regularly referenced Palestinians in his writing, most consistently in his book *A Little Matter of Genocide: Holocaust and Denial in the Americas 1492 to the Present* (San Francisco: City Lights, 2001). Churchill largely focuses on the physical violence of the United States and Israel, paying little note to discursive comparison. Norman Finkelstein has a comparative chapter on the Cherokee and Palestinians in *The Rise and Fall of Palestine: A Personal Account of the Intifada Years* (Minneapolis: University of Minnesota Press, 1996). Although conceptually solid, Finkelstein's comparison is problematic because it overlooks various American Indian sources.

2. See Robert Warrior, "Canaanites, Cowboys, and Indians: Deliverance, Conquest, and Liberation Theology Today," *Christianity and Crisis* (September 11, 1989): 261–65. Warrior presented an update of this paper at the 2011 Native American and Indigenous Studies Association (NAISA) conference in Sacramento, examining Natives and Palestinians in comparative context more explicitly than he does in the original essay. Former AIM leader Russell Means once proclaimed, "What the American Indian Movement says is that the American Indians are the Palestinians of the United States, and the Palestinians are the American Indians of the Middle East." See http://www.counterpunch.org/2009/01/12/russell-means-breaks-the-silence-on-obama/.

3. Frantz Fanon, *The Wretched of the Earth,* reprint edition, trans. Richard Philcox (New York: Grove Press, 2005), 2.

4. Ibid.

5. "Towards a National Indian Literature," in Jace Weaver, Craig S. Womack, and Robert Warrior, *American Indian Literary Nationalism* (Albuquerque: University of New Mexico Press, 2006), 259.

6. Ibid., xv.

7. The 2016 NAISA annual meeting took place in Honolulu and featured considerable interchange among Palestinian attendees and Native Hawaiians.

8. The Palestinian claim to "Indigenous" status at the UN has generally been connected to the Bedouin (traditional, nomadic, tribal communities), though Palestinians have also worked to include the whole of Palestinian society in the category.

1. How Palestine Became Important to American Indian Studies

1. Warrior writes at length of his days as Said's student in his section of Jace Weaver, Craig S. Womack, and Robert Warrior, *American Indian Literary Nationalism* (Albuquerque: University of New Mexico Press, 2006).

2. I refer to McNickle's sense of tribalism as the cultural orientations that define who is Native. See Darcy McNickle, *Native American Tribalism: Indian Survivals and Renewals* (Oxford and New York: Oxford University Press, 2003).

3. Warrior writes of his days as Said's student in *American Indian Literary Nationalism*.

4. See www.usacbi.org.

5. Neferti X. M. Tadiar, "Why the Question of Palestine Is a Feminist Concern," *Social Text* (February 15, 2012), http://www.socialtextjournal.org/blog/2012/02/why-the-question-of-palestine-is-a-feminist-concern.php.

6. J. Kēhaulani Kauanui, "One Occupation," *Social Text* (July 5, 2012), http://www.socialtextjournal.org/periscope/2012/07/one-occupation.php.

7. See Perry Miller, *Errand into the Wilderness* (Cambridge: Harvard University Press, 1956); and Sacvan Berkovitch, *The Puritan Origins of the American Self*, reissue edition (New Haven: Yale University Press, 2011).

8. See Hilton Obenzinger, *American Palestine* (Princeton, N.J.: Princeton University Press, 1999).

9. See Orly Benjamin, "Roots of the Neoliberal Takeover in Israel," *Challenge* (July/August 2008), http://www.challenge-mag.com/en/article__224/roots_of_the_neoliberal_takeover_in_israel; and Adam

Jones, *Genocide: A Comprehensive Introduction,* 2d ed. (London: Routledge, 2010), 147.

10. See Jodi Byrd, *The Transit of Empire: Indigenous Critiques of Colonialism* (Minneapolis: University of Minnesota Press, 2011); Jasbir Puar, *Terrorist Assemblages: Homonationalism in Queer Times* (Durham, N.C.: Duke University Press, 2007); and Scott Lauria Morgensen, *Spaces between Us: Queer Settler Colonialism and Indigenous Colonization* (Minneapolis: University of Minnesota Press, 2011).

11. The New York Police Department, for example, opened a branch in Israel in 2012, ten years after having received formal training in policing practices from Israel's military-intelligence apparatus. See http://nymag.com/daily/intelligencer/2012/09/nypd-now-has-an-israel-branch.html.

12. Jimmy Johnson and Linda Quiquivix, "Israel and Mexico Swap Notes on Abusing Rights," *Electronic Intifada* (May 21, 2013), http://electronicintifada.net/content/israel-and-mexico-swap-notes-abusing-rights/12475.

13. The line is quoted from a 2009 Marcos speech archived at http://mywordismyweapon.blogspot.com/2009/01/of-sowing-and-harvests-subcomandante.html.

14. See Philip Taubman, "Israel Said to Aid Latin Aims of U.S.," *New York Times,* July 21, 1983, http://www.nytimes.com/1983/07/21/world/israel-said-to-aid-latin-aims-of-us.html.

15. Irin Carmon, "Linked Arms," *Tablet,* February 21, 2012, http://www.tabletmag.com/jewish-news-and-politics/91666/linked-arms.

16. Ibid.

17. Robert Parry, "Ariel Sharon and Israel's Hand in Guatemala's Genocide," Global Research, January 17, 2014, http://www.globalresearch.ca/israels-hand-in-guatemalas-genocide/5336243.

18. Justin Elliott, "WikiLeaks' Revealing Information about U.S. Citizens Living in West Bank," Salon, August 24, 2011, http://www.salon.com/2011/08/24/wikileaks_us_citizens_west_bank/.

19. Raphael Ahren, "The American Settler You Don't Know," *Ha'aretz,* October 7, 2011, http://www.haaretz.com/weekend/anglo-file/the-american-settler-you-don-t-know-1.388640.

20. Ibid.

21. Luke Laeser, "Project 365 — Climbing Devils Tower Every Day for a Year," *Climbing* (undated — accessed on July 13, 2015), http://www.climbing.com/climber/project-365-climbing-devils-tower-every-day-for-a-year/.

22. Laeser's article explains: "An annual voluntary climbing ban occurs in June on Devils Tower that many folks comply with. Others, like

Frank, find the tower to be a sacred place in their own belief system and see that climbing can be a sacred activity as well. Frank hoped to unite the many people who find Devils Tower a sacred place in aiding the Native Americans in the region. As Frank puts it: 'This is not *El Cap in 2.5 Hours.* It's more like *Three Cups of Tea* and it is what one soul has been doing for his 57th year on this planet.' His 'not-for-profit' organization is www.devilstower-sacredtomanypeople.org."

23. This narrative played out in a controversial 2010 Columbia University conference sponsored by its Institute for Israel and Jewish Studies and Institute for Religion, Culture and Public Life. "In this conference," organizers announced, "we hope to address some of the rich, timely and thought-provoking connections between Jews and Native Americans, both discursive and actual." Some Natives and Palestinians criticized the conference for its explicit and implicit Zionist focus.

24. See http://www.utexas.edu/cola/inits/nais/.

25. See http://www.ais.arizona.edu/content/mission-and-core-values.

26. A full video and transcript of the speech can be found at http://www.whitehouse.gov/photos-and-video/video/2012/03/04/president-obama-2012-aipac-policy-conference.

27. Chemi Salev, "Hagel: 'I Intend to Expand the Depth and Breadth of U.S.–Israel Cooperation,'" *Ha'aretz,* January 15, 2013, http://www.haaretz.com/news/diplomacy-defense/hagel-i-intend-to-expand-the-depth-and-breadth-of-u-s-israel-cooperation.premium-1.494075. As a senator, Hagel reliably voted for both pro-Israel and anti-Palestinian legislation. For more information about his voting record and professions of support for Israel, see http://jstreet.org/the-facts-on-chuck-hagel#proisrael.

28. J. Kēhaulani Kuaunai, "Ethical Questions of Boycotting Israel," in *Shifting Borders: America and the Middle East/North Africa,* ed. Alex Lubin (Beirut and New York: American University of Beirut Press, forthcoming).

29. Irwin Cotler, "The Gathering Storm, and Beyond," *Jerusalem Post,* May 14, 2008, http://www.jpost.com/Opinion/Op-EdContributors/Article.aspx?id=101152.

30. A number of scholarly books have shown that Zionism's claims to an ancient Jewish past in Palestine are largely mythological. See Shlomo Sand, *The Invention of the Land of Israel: From Holy Land to Homeland,* trans. Geremy Forman (London: Verso, 2012); Keith Whitelam, *The Invention of Ancient Israel: The Silencing of Palestinian History* (London and New York: Routledge, 1997); and Eyal Weizman, *Hollow Land: Israel's Architecture of Occupation* (London: Verso, 2012).

31. Allen Z. Hertz, "Aboriginal Rights of the Jewish People," *American Thinker*, October 30, 2011, http://www.americanthinker.com/articles/2011/10/aboriginal_rights_of_the_jewish_people.html.

32. New England Committee to Defend Palestine, "A Short History of the Colonization of Palestine," online pamphlet (in pdf) available at http://www.onepalestine.org/resources/flyers/MythHistory.pdf; accessed July 13, 2015.

33. Laila Al-Marayati, "Will Palestinians Go the Way of Native Americans?" *Los Angeles Times,* April 21, 2002, http://articles.latimes.com/2002/apr/21/opinion/op-almarayati.rtf.

34. Quoted in Nathan Thrall, "Feeling Good about Feeling Bad," *London Review of Books,* October 9, 2014.

35. Stephen P. Gasteyer and Cornelia Butler Flora, "Modernizing the Savage: Colonization and Perceptions of Landscape and Lifescape," *Sociologica Ruralis* 40:1 (2000): 134.

36. Tim Giago, "Israel Could Have Learned Much from Native Americans," *Notes from Indian Country,* August 22, 2005, http://www.nativetimes.com/index.asp?action=displayarticle&article_id=6881.

37. Steven T. Newcomb, *Pagans in the Promised Land: Decoding the Doctrine of Discovery* (Golden, Colo.: Fulcrum Publishing, 2008), xxii.

38. Duane Champagne and Ismael Abu-Saad, "Introduction," in *Future of Indigenous People: Strategies for Survival and Development,* ed. Duane Champagne and Ismael Abu-Saad (Los Angeles: UCLA American Indian Studies Center, 2003), x.

2. Boycotting Israel as Native Nationalism

1. "Netanyahu's AIPAC Speech: The Full Transcript," *Ha'aretz,* March 4, 2014, http://www.haaretz.com/news/diplomacy-defense/1.577920.

2. Major differences include the breadth of the South African boycott, which achieved participation of states and wealthy governing bodies, something that at this point seems inconceivable vis-à-vis BDS, and the trenchant relationship of antiapartheid activism to a particular set of racial issues that resonated in the United States.

3. See, for example, Ali Abunimah, *The Battle for Justice in Palestine* (Chicago: Haymarket, 2014).

4. The Palestinian Authority, for instance, has arrested BDS activists. See Jake Wallis Simons, "Why Even the Palestinian Authority Opposes the Boycott of Israel," *Telegraph,* June 9, 2014, http://blogs.telegraph.co.uk/news/jakewallissimons/100275416/israels-enemies-are-dealt-a-heavy-blow-by-the-palestinian-authority/. Simons is incorrect that the

184 • Notes to Chapter 2

PA formally opposes the boycott. All major Palestinian political parties have, as of this writing, endorsed BDS. Throughout the Arab world, however, suppression of Palestinian nationalism has long been an informal (and sometimes formal) rule.

5. Reggae legend Peter Tosh, for instance, was boycotting Israel as early as the late 1970s. See Ian Burrell, "Move over Bob Marley: Peter Tosh Is Finally Getting the Recognition He Deserves," *Independent*, November 2, 2012, http://www.independent.co.uk/arts-entertainment/music/features/move-over-bob-marley-peter-tosh-is-finally-getting-the-recognition-he-deserves-8914028.html.

6. In June 2015, Republican financier Sheldon Adelson held a secret anti-BDS summit in conjunction with Democratic financier Haim Saban. Together they raised almost $50 million to battle BDS. See Nathan Guttman, "Secret Sheldon Adelson Summit Raises up to $50M for Strident Anti-BDS Push," *Forward*, June 9, 2015, http://forward.com/news/israel/309676/secret-sheldon-adelson-summit-raises-up-to-50m-for-strident-anti-bds-push/.

7. See Ron Gerlitz and Jabir Asaqla, "Discrimination against Israeli Arabs Still Rampant, 10 Years On," *Ha'aretz*, October 2, 2013, http://www.haaretz.com/opinion/.premium-1.550152.

8. Peter Beinart often uses this type of argument. See his article "The Real Problem with the American Studies Association's Boycott of Israel," Daily Beast, December 17, 2013, http://www.thedailybeast.com/articles/2013/12/17/the-american-studies-association-is-really-boycotting-israel-s-existence.html.

9. See, for example, David Greenberg, "The ASA's Boycott of Israel Is Not as Troubling as It Seems," *New Republic*, December 19, 2013, http://www.newrepublic.com/article/115995/asas-boycott-israel-not-troubling-it-seems.

10. Jeremy Suri, for example, frets, "Unfortunately, the ASA has decided that it should now condemn the state of Israel, exclude Israeli institutions, and ostracize those scholars and students who come from Israel or feel some religious, cultural, or political association with Israel" ("Intolerance, Boycotts, and the ASA," Academe Blog, December 20, 2013, http://academeblog.org/2013/12/20/intolerance-boycotts-and-the-asa/.

11. See Ashley Dawson and Bill V. Mullen, eds., *Against Apartheid: The Case for Boycotting Israeli Universities* (Chicago: Haymarket, 2015).

12. See Michael Berube, "Boycott Bubkes," Al Jazeera America, January 8, 2014, http://america.aljazeera.com/opinions/2014/1/boycott-asa-israelbds.html.

13. The Anti-Defamation League (ADL), for example, sent a letter of protest to the AAAS, available here: http://www.adl.org/israel-inter national/anti-israel-activity/c/adl-urges-association-for.html. The AAAS resolution passed on April 20, 2013. Its text can be found at http://www .aaastudies.org/content/images/files/aaas%204_20_13%20-%20confer ence%20resolution%20to%20support%20the%20boycott%20of%20 israeli%20academic%20institutions.pdf.

14. Beinart, "The Real Problem with the American Studies Association's Boycott of Israel."

15. In a debate I had in 2013 with Beinart on Marc Steiner's WEAA (Baltimore) radio program, Beinart confessed that he's more concerned with the maintenance of a Jewish majority than he is with actual democracy.

16. For a good overview of racism among Israeli politicians, see Mazal Mualem, "Anti-Arab Racism Becomes Tool in Israeli Elections," trans. Simon Pompan, al-Monitor, February 10, 2015, http://www.al-mon itor.com/pulse/originals/2015/02/israel-elections-2015-racism-arabs-right -wing-bennett.html#.

17. While there is significant overlap between American Indian stud ies (AIS) and ethnic studies, broadly conceived, it would appear that most AIS practitioners prefer disciplinary autonomy based on the primacy of nationalism in Native thought and practice.

18. Quoted in Sean Savage, "American Studies Professors: Israel Boy cott Antithetical to Values of Academia," JNS.org, December 18, 2013, http://www.jns.org/latest-articles/2013/12/18/american-studies-profes sors-israel-boycott-antithetical-to-scholarly-pursuits#.VaR4JvmIJ2g=.

19. Slotkin proffered these observations on December 17, 2013, in the comments section of the ASA Web site, which is archived on the Middle East Children's Alliance (MECA) Web site: https://www.mecafor peace.org/news/asa-members-vote-endorse-academic-boycott-israel.

20. Perhaps the worst example arises from former Israeli ambassador to the United States Michael Oren, who said of Marez, "ASA President Curtis Marez, who defended the selection of the Jewish state for his organi zation's first-ever boycott by saying 'one has to start somewhere,' has been especially denounced as anti-Semitic in effect if not intention" (Politico, December 20, 2013, http://www.politico.com/magazine/story/2013/12/will -congress-stand-up-for-academic-freedom-101379.html#.VaR73_mIJ2g).

21. See Steven Salaita, "Politico refuses to publish rebuttal of Michael Oren's anti-Semitism smear," Electronic Intifada, February 19, 2014, https://electronicintifada.net/blogs/steven-salaita/politico-refuses-publish -rebuttal-michael-orens-anti-semitism-smear.

22. Richard Behar, "Open Letter to NYU's President: Why the American Studies Assn.'s Israel Boycott Makes Me Ashamed to Be an Alumnus," Forbes, January 14, 2014, http://www.forbes.com/sites/richardbehar/2014/01/14/open-letter-to-nyus-president-why-the-american-studies-assn-s-israel-boycott-makes-me-ashamed-to-be-an-alumnus/.

23. In South Africa, Abbas declared, "But we ask everyone to boycott the products of the settlements. Because the settlements are in our territories. It is illegal. . . . But we don't ask anyone to boycott Israel itself. We have relations with Israel, we have mutual recognition of Israel." See Ali Abunimah, "In South Africa, Abbas opposes boycott of Israel," Electronic Intifada, December 12, 2013, https://electronicintifada.net/blogs/ali-abunimah/south-africa-abbas-opposes-boycott-israel.

24. Alyosha Goldstein, "Toward a Genealogy of the U.S. Colonial Present," in Formations of United States Colonialism, ed. Alyosha Goldstein (Durham, N.C.: Duke University Press, 2014), 2.

25. Jennifer Nez Denetdale, "'I'm Not Running on My Gender': The 2010 Navajo Nation Presidential Race, Gender, and the Politics of Tradition," in Goldstein, Formations of United States Colonialism, 318.

26. Ibid.

27. Jodi Byrd, The Transit of Empire (Minneapolis: University of Minnesota Press, 2011), xvi–xvii.

28. Ibid., xix.

29. Kevin Bruyneel, The Third Space of Sovereignty: The Postcolonial Politics of U.S.–Indigenous Relations (Minneapolis: University of Minnesota Press, 2007), xvii.

30. Glen Coulthard, Red Skin, White Masks: Rejecting the Colonial Politics of Recognition (Minneapolis: University of Minnesota Press, 2014).

31. Iris Marion Young, Global Challenges: War, Self-Determination, and Responsibility for Justice (Malden, Mass., and Cambridge: Polity, 2007), 16–17.

32. Omar Barghouti, Boycott, Divestment, Sanctions: The Global Struggle for Palestinian Rights (Chicago: Haymarket, 2011), 104.

33. Mike Krebs and Dana M. Olwan, "'From Jerusalem to the Grand River, Our Struggles Are One': Challenging Canadian and Israeli Settler Colonialism," Settler Colonial Studies 2:2 (2013): 157.

34. They write: "it is now common to invite indigenous allies to speak at Palestine events. While we believe this is an important and necessary turn, we are concerned that the inclusion of indigenous spokespersons at Palestine solidarity events can, at times, be tokenistic" (ibid., 158).

35. Ibid., 143–44.

36. Mishuana Goeman, *Mark My Words: Native Women Mapping Our Nations* (Minneapolis: University of Minnesota Press, 2013), 2.

37. Waziyatawin, "Malice Enough in Their Hearts and Courage Enough in Ours: Reflections on US Indigenous and Palestinian Experiences under Occupation," *Settler Colonial Studies* 2:1 (2013): 173.

38. Ibid., 177.

39. Ibid., 180.

40. Joseph Massad, "Recognizing Palestine, BDS and the Survival of Israel," Electronic Intifada, December 16, 2014, http://electronicinti fada.net/content/recognizing-palestine-bds-and-survival-israel/14123.

41. Judith Butler, "Academic Freedom and the ASA's Boycott of Israel: A Response to Michelle Goldberg," *Nation,* December 8, 2013, http://www.thenation.com/article/177512/academic-freedom-and-asas -boycott-israel-response-michelle-goldberg#.

42. Find the full statement here: http://www.naisa.org/declaration -of-support-for-the-boycott-of-israeli-academic-institutions.html.

43. J. Kēhaulani Kauanui, "One Occupation," *Social Text,* July 5, 2012, http://socialtextjournal.org/periscope_article/one_occupation/.

3. Ethnic Cleansing as National Uplift

1. Steven Newcomb, "The Old Testament Religious Basis of U.S. Federal Indian Law and Policy," *Indian Country Today Media Network,* January 22, 2015, http://indiancountrytodaymedianetwork.com/2015/ 01/22/old-testament-religious-basis-us-federal-indian-law-and-policy.

2. The Second Annual Message is available at the following link: http://www.digitalhistory.uh.edu/active_learning/explorations/indian_ removal/jackson_second_address.cfm.

3. The First Annual Message is available at the following link: http://www.digitalhistory.uh.edu/active_learning/explorations/indian_ removal/jackson_first_address.cfm.

4. Dale Turner, *This Is Not a Peace Pipe* (Toronto: University of Toronto Press, 2006), 96.

5. Jodi Byrd, *The Transit of Empire* (Minneapolis: University of Minnesota Press, 2011), xv.

6. The Sixth Annual Message is available at the following link: http://www.digitalhistory.uh.edu/active_learning/explorations/indian_ removal/jackson_sixth_address.cfm.

7. The Fifth Annual Message is available at the following link: http://www.digitalhistory.uh.edu/active_learning/explorations/indian_ removal/jackson_fifth_address.cfm.

8. Avi Shlaim, *The Iron Wall: Israel and the Arab World* (New York: W. W. Norton, 2001), 598.

9. I use a version of "The Iron Wall" available at the following link: http://www.marxists.de/middleast/ironwall/ironwall.htm.

10. See Avi Shlaim, *Collusion across the Jordan: King Abdullah, the Zionist Movement, and the Partition of Palestine* (New York: Columbia University Press, 1988); Nur Masalha, *Expulsion of the Palestinians: The Concept of "Transfer" in Zionist Political Thought, 1882–1948* (Washington, D.C.: Institute for Palestine Studies, 1992); and Ilan Pappe, *The Ethnic Cleansing of Palestine* (London: Oneworld Publications, 2007).

11. Gyasi Ross, "Why I, as a Native American, Support the Palestinian People," *Progressive,* June 25, 2002, http://www.progressive.org/media_1530.

12. Ibid.

13. Walter Mignolo, "Delinking: The Rhetoric of Modernity, the Logic of Coloniality, and the Grammar of De-Coloniality," in *I Am Where I Think: Globalization and the De-Colonial Option* (Durham, N.C.: Duke University Press, 2008), 8.

14. Ibid.

15. Quoted in Gonzalez Kuehner Hebert and Ragina Johnson, "Common Struggles Half a World Apart," *Socialist Worker,* August 7, 2014, http://socialistworker.org/2014/08/07/common-struggles-half-a-world-apart.

16. Barak Ravid, "White House Responds to Netanyahu: American Values Gave Israel the Iron Dome," *Ha'aretz,* October 7, 2014, http://www.haaretz.com/news/diplomacy-defense/1.619534.

17. Harsha Walia, "'Land Is a Relationship': In Conversation with Glen Coulthard on Indigenous Nationhood," *Rabble.ca,* January 21, 2015, http://rabble.ca/columnists/2015/01/land-relationship-conversation-glen-coulthard-on-indigenous-nationhood.

4. Inter/National Aesthetics

1. Lee Maracle, "On the AFN Visit to Palestine," January 1, 2006. Archived at the Canada Palestine Association Web site: http://www.cpavancouver.org/index.php/2006/01/01/lee-maracle-to-the-afn/.

2. Erica Violet Lee, "Our Revolution: First Nations Women in Solidarity with Palestine," *Moontime Warrior,* August 19, 2014, http://moontimewarrior.com/2014/08/19/our-revolution-first-nations-women-in-solidarity-with-palestine/.

3. I use the version of the poem displayed on Lee's blog, listed at the link in the preceding note.

4. The lyrics to "Rich Man's War" are available at http://www.lyrics.com/rich-mans-war-lyrics-john-trudell.html.

5. Carter Revard, "A Response to Terrorists," in *An Eagle Nation* (Tucson: University of Arizona Press, 1993), 101–2.

6. Said's seminal essay "Zionism from the Standpoint of Its Victims" illuminates these complexities (*Social Text* [winter 1979]: 7–58).

7. Lee Maracle, "Song to a Palestinian Child," in *Bent Box* (Penticon, B.C.: Theytus, 2000), 33.

8. Arafat's speech can be found in its entirety at the following link: http://www.al-bab.com/arab/docs/pal/arafat_gun_and_olive_branch.htm.

9. Edgar Gabriel Silex, *Acts of Love* (Willimantic, Conn.: Curbstone Press, 2004). 33.

10. The poem is often translated as "The Speech of the Red Indian," but I use Fady Joudah's translation, which is available in the *Harvard Review* 36 (2009): 152–59.

11. All passages are quoted from the Joudah translation cited in note 10.

12. Means's poem is posted in the comments section of The Corner Report blog, available at http://www.thecornerreport.com/index.php?p=3456&more=1&c=1&tb=1&pb=1. I have confirmed with the blog's proprietor that the post was indeed made by Means.

5. Why American Indian Studies Should Be Important to Palestine Solidarity

1. Keith P. Feldman, *A Shadow over Palestine: The Imperial Life of Race in America* (Minneapolis: University of Minnesota Press, 2015), 35–36.

2. See Walid Khalidi, *Palestine Reborn* (London: I. B. Tauris, 1992); and Fayez Sayegh, *Zionist Colonialism in Palestine* (Beirut: Research Center, Palestine Liberation Organization, 1965).

3. See Nadera Shalhoub-Kevorkian, "Human Suffering in Colonial Contexts: Reflections from Palestine," *Settler Colonial Studies* (2014), http://www.tandfonline.com/doi/full/10.1080/2201473X.2013.859979; and Magid Shihade, "Not Just a Picnic: Settler Colonialism, Mobility, and Identity among Palestinians in Israel," *Biography* 37:2 (2014): 451–73.

4. The complete statement can be found on the AIS Web site: http://www.ais.illinois.edu/mascot/.

5. The entire report is available at the AAUP Web site: http://www.aaup.org/report/UIUC.

6. Vicente M. Diaz, "The Salaita Case and Cary Nelson's Use of 'Academic Freedom' to Silence Dissent," Electronic Intifada, August 14,

2014, http://electronicintifada.net/content/salaita-case-and-cary-nelsons
-use-academic-freedom-silence-dissent/13756.

7. Glen Sean Coulthard, *Red Skin, White Masks: Rejecting the Colonial Politics of Recognition* (Minneapolis: University of Minnesota Press, 2014), x.

8. Penelope Kelsey, "Gathering the Threads Together: Comparative Urban/Rural/Diasporic/Multitribal Nationalisms," in *Comparative Indigeneities of the Americas: Toward a Hemispheric Approach*, ed. M. Bianet Castellanos, Lourdes Gutierrez Najera, and Arturo J. Aldama (Tucson: University of Arizona Press, 2012), 29.

9. Ibid., 23–24.

10. Audra Simpson, *Mohawk Interruptus: Political Life across the Borders of Settler States* (Durham, N.C.: Duke University Press, 2014), 11.

11. Chadwick Allen, *Trans-Indigenous: Methodologies for Global Native Literary Studies* (Minneapolis: University of Minnesota Press, 2012), xxxii.

12. Patrick Wolfe, "Settler Colonialism and the Elimination of the Native," *Journal of Genocide Research* 8:4 (2006): 389.

13. Ibid., 394.

14. John Collins, *Global Palestine* (New York: Columbia University Press, 2011), x.

15. Ibid., 6.

16. Ibid., 8.

17. Mark Rifkin, "Indigeneity, Apartheid, Palestine: On the Transit of Political Metaphors," *Cultural Critique,* forthcoming.

18. Jennifer Heath, *"The Map Is Not the Territory": Parallel Paths—Palestinians, Native Americans, Irish* (Boulder, Colo.: Baksun Books and Arts, 2015), 15.

19. Ibid.

20. Jordan Skinner, "The Indians of Palestine: An Interview between Gilles Deleuze and Elias Sanbar," Verso Blog, August 8, 2014, http://www.versobooks.com/blogs/1684-the-indians-of-palestine-an-interview-between-gilles-deleuze-and-elias-sanbar.

21. Ibid.

22. See Magid Shihade, *Not Just a Soccer Game: Colonialism and Conflict among Palestinians in Israel* (Syracuse, N.Y.: Syracuse University Press, 2011).

23. Skinner, "The Indians of Palestine."

24. Ibid.

25. Gyasi Ross, "Why I, as a Native American, Support the Palestinian People," *Progressive,* June 25, 2002, http://progressive.org/media_1530.

26. Ibid.

27. Ibid.

28. James Cairns, "Why Are the Harper Conservatives So Pro-Israel?" *New Socialist,* May 13, 2013, http://www.newsocialist.org/695-why-are -the-harper-conservatives-so-pro-israel.

29. Max Blumenthal, "Shocking 'Extermination' Fantasies by the People Running America's Empire on Full Display at Aspen Summit," AlterNet, July 25, 2013, http://www.alternet.org/tea-party-and-right/shocking -extermination-fantasies-people-running-americas-empire-full-display.

30. Alex Kane, "Shared Values: Likud Member Says Prawer Plan Akin to What 'Americans Did to the Indians,'" MondoWeiss, December 11, 2013, http://mondoweiss.net/2013/12/prawer-americans-indians.

31. Annie Robbins, "Moe Diab: Prawer Plan Recalls Historical Atrocity of Native American Ethnic Cleansing," MondoWeiss, July 26, 2013, http://mondoweiss.net/2013/07/moe-diab-prawer-plan-recalls-historical -atrocity-of-native-american-ethnic-cleansing.

32. Antonia Zerbisias, "Canadian Aboriginal Activist Stands Up to Israel," Al Jazeera, June 26, 2015, http://www.aljazeera.com/indepth/opin ion/2015/06/canadian-aboriginal-activist-stands-israel-gaza-15062607 3951799.html.

33. "Bob Lovelace, Canadian Delegate to Freedom Flotilla III," *Beit Zatoun,* June 14, 2015, http://beitzatoun.org/event/sailing-to-gaza-again/.

34. Quoted from an *Arab Talk* radio program with Jess Ghannam. Archive available at https://archive.org/details/ProfessorKehaulaniKauanui OnPlaestine.

Conclusion

1. Blake Eskin, "Like Monopoly in the Depression, Settlers of Catan Is the Board Game of Our Time," *Washington Post,* November 21, 2010, http://www.washingtonpost.com/wp-dyn/content/article/2010/11/24/AR 2010112404140.html.

2. See the company's Web site: http://www.catan.com/game/settlers -canaan.

3. http://www.catan.com/game/settlers-america-trails-rails.

INDEX

∎ ∎ ∎

BDS and, 48–49, 56–57; colonization in, 1, 89, 95; corporate media and, 168; El Salvador and, 113; erosion of, 119, 167; as global issue, 6, 119, 166; Indigenous studies and, 143, 167, 169; Israeli domination of, 10, 18, 160; Native history and, 167; Native poets and, 104, 105, 106–7, 132; poetic intervention into, 106; spatial dynamics of, 168; statehood for, 67; in the world, 152–56; Zionism and, 154

Palestine Liberation Organization (PLO), 9, 57

Palestine Research Center, 135

Palestine solidarity, 64, 132, 134, 135, 136, 142, 143, 144, 147, 152, 162; AIS and, 164–71; importance of, 145–46

Palestine studies, 15, 24, 132, 135, 136

Palestinian Academic and Cultural Boycott of Israel (PACBI), 29, 30, 34

Palestinian Authority (PA), 34, 57, 67

Palestinian liberation, 4, 134, 135, 136, 171

Palestinians, xviii, 12, 13, 15, 22, 33, 40, 46, 49, 55, 56, 83, 160, 165, 166; acknowledgment for, 164; ancestral land and, 124; attacks on, 123; colonization and, 43; decolonization and, xvii, 3, 176; dialogue and, 44; diasporic, 30; discrimination against, 8, 10, 68; dispossession

of, 20, 65; existence of, 18; Hawaiians and, xvii; as Indigenous people, 156, 180n8; interactions with, 145; Jews and, 35, 74, 88, 93; liberation and, 16; massacres of, 20; Natives and, x, xv, xvii, xix, 2, 4, 15, 17, 24, 84, 89, 95, 100, 103, 105, 117, 121, 122, 128, 131, 143, 159, 162, 163, 176; refugee camps and, 43; study of, 169; U.S. settlement and, 64; Zionism and, 19, 74, 89, 90–91

Palestinian students/academics, 56, 67; boycott and, 48; subordination of, 36

Pappe, Ilan, 46

Patagonia: Palestine and, 22

patriarchy, 60, 65, 106

patriotism, xvi, 59

pedagogy, xvi, 38–39

peoplehood, xvii, 148, 154, 157

People's Movement Assembly, 153

Perez, Shimon: human dignity and, 16

personhood, 81, 93, 109, 112, 149

Pine Ridge Reservation, 110, 111, 112

Plan Dalet, 94

PLO. See Palestine Liberation Organization

plutocracy, xvi, 8, 9, 116, 141, 147, 167, 170

poetry, Native, 103, 104, 105, 106–7

political commitment, 24, 38, 121

politics, 2, 4, 23, 55, 58, 108, 126, 132, 154, 169; class, 148;

Steven Salaita is Edward W. Said Chair of American Studies at the American University of Beirut. *Inter/Nationalism* is his eighth book.